Experiencing Choral Music

PROFICIENT

TREBLE

P9-EML-702

Developed by

HAL•LEONARD® CORPORATION

McGraw Hill Glencoe

New York, New York   Columbus, Ohio   Chicago, Illinois   Peoria, Illinois   Woodland Hills, California

The portions of the National Standards for Music Education included here are reprinted from National Standards for Arts Education with permission from MENC—The National Association for Music Education. All rights reserved. Copyright © 1994 by MENC. The complete National Standards and additional materials relating to the Standards are available from MENC, 1806 Robert Fulton Drive, Reston, VA 20191 (telephone 800-336-3768).

A portion of the sales of this material goes to support music education programs through programs of MENC—The National Association for Music Education.

 **Glencoe**

The **McGraw·Hill** Companies

Printed in the United States of America.

Send all inquiries to:
Glencoe/McGraw-Hill
21600 Oxnard Street, Suite 500
Woodland Hills, CA 91367

ISBN 0-07-861122-9 (Student Edition)
ISBN 0-07-861123-7 (Teacher Wraparound Edition)

   5 6 7 8 9   045   09 08 07

Credits

LEAD AUTHORS

Emily Crocker
Vice President of Choral Publications
Hal Leonard Corporation, Milwaukee, Wisconsin
Founder and Artistic Director, Milwaukee Children's Choir

Michael Jothen
Professor of Music, Program Director of Graduate Music Education
Chairperson of Music Education
Towson University, Towson, Maryland

Jan Juneau
Choral Director
Klein Collins High School
Spring, Texas

Henry H. Leck
Associate Professor and Director of Choral Activities
Butler University, Indianapolis, Indiana
Founder and Artistic Director, Indianapolis Children's Choir

Michael O'Hern
Choral Director
Lake Highlands High School
Richardson, Texas

Audrey Snyder
Composer
Eugene, Oregon

Mollie Tower
Coordinator of Choral and General Music, K-12, Retired
Austin, Texas

AUTHORS

Anne Denbow
Voice Instructor, Professional Singer/Actress
Director of Music, Holy Cross Episcopal Church
Simpsonville, South Carolina

Rollo A. Dilworth
Director of Choral Activities and Music
   Education
North Park University, Chicago, Illinois

Deidre Douglas
Choral Director
Labay Junior High, Katy, Texas

Ruth E. Dwyer
Associate Director and Director of Education
Indianapolis Children's Choir
Indianapolis, Indiana

Norma Freeman
Choral Director
Saline High School, Saline, Michigan

Cynthia I. Gonzales
Music Theorist
Greenville, South Carolina

Michael Mendoza
Professor of Choral Activities
New Jersey State University
Trenton, New Jersey

Thomas Parente
Associate Professor
Westminster Choir College of Rider University
Princeton, New Jersey

Barry Talley
Director of Fine Arts and Choral Director
Deer Park ISD, Deer Park, Texas

CONTRIBUTING AUTHORS

Debbie Daniel
Choral Director, Webb Middle School
Garland, Texas

Roger Emerson
Composer/Arranger
Mount Shasta, California

Kari Gilbertson
Choral Director, Forest Meadow Junior High
Richardson, Texas

Tim McDonald
Creative Director, Music Theatre International
New York, New York

Christopher W. Peterson
Assistant Professor of Music Education (Choral)
University of Wisconsin-Milwaukee
Milwaukee, Wisconsin

Kirby Shaw
Composer/Arranger
Ashland, Oregon

Stephen Zegree
Professor of Music
Western Michigan State University
Kalamazoo, Michigan

EDITORIAL

Linda Rann
Senior Editor
Hal Leonard Corporation
Milwaukee, Wisconsin

Stacey Nordmeyer
Choral Editor
Hal Leonard Corporation
Milwaukee, Wisconsin

Table of Contents

Introductory Materials . . . . i-viii

Lessons

1   **In Time Of Silver Rain • SSA** 2
    Audrey Snyder

    Spotlight On Posture & Breath Management 9

2   **Shiru • 2-Part** 10
    Allan E. Naplan

3   **Didn't My Lord Deliver Daniel • SSA** 20
    Traditional Spiritual, arranged by Ken Berg

4   **The Star-Spangled Banner • SSAA** 32
    John Stafford Smith, arranged by Barry Talley

5   **Homeland • SSA** 36
    Gustav Holst, arranged by Z. Randall Stroope

6   **Domine File Unigenite • SSA** 48
    Giovanni Pierluigi da Palestrina,
    edited by Matthew Michaels

7   **Through Winter's Window • SSA** 56
    Brad Printz

    Spotlight On Physiology Of The Voice 65

8   **Go Where I Send Thee! • SSA** 66
    Gospel Spiritual, arranged by Paul Caldwell & Sean Ivory

    Spotlight On Gospel Music 75

9   **Vere Languores Nostros • SSA** 76
    Antonio Lotti, arranged by Thomas Juneau

10 **Overture To *Die Zauberflöte* • SSAA** 82
    Wolfgang Amadeus Mozart, arranged by Arkadi Serper

    Spotlight On Physiology Of Singing 93

11   **Die Schwestern (The Sisters) • SA** 94
Johannes Brahms, edited by Judith Blezzard

12   **Fire • 3-Part Treble** 104
Mary Goetze

Spotlight On Concert Etiquette 114

Music & History

Renaissance Period 116

Baroque Period 120

Classical Period 124

Romantic Period 128

Contemporary Period 132

Spotlight On Careers In Music 136

Choral Library

Ah! si mon moine voulait danser! • SSAA 138
French Canadian Folk Song, arranged by Donald Patriquin

Spotlight On Arranging 151

El Pambiche Lento • 2-Part 152
Dominican Republic Folk Merengue,
arranged by Juan-Tony Guzmán

He's Gone Away • SSA 170
American Folk Song, arranged by Ron Nelson

Hoj, Hura, Hoj • SSAA 176
Moravian Czech Mountain Song, arranged by Otma Mácha

Spotlight On Vocal Health 185

Music Down In My Soul • SSA 186
African American Spiritual, arranged by Moses Hogan

O Vos Omnes • SSAA 198
Thomas Juneau

Spotlight On Improvisation 203

Psalm 100 • SSA 204
René Clausen

Sebben, crudele • 2-Part 220
Antonio Caldara, arranged by Henry Leck

Spotlight On Vocal Jazz 231

See The Gipsies • SSAA 232
Hungarian Folk Song, arranged by Zoltán Kodály

Sing A New Song • SSAA 240
Michael D. Mendoza

Sing A Song of Sixpence • SA 246
Michael D. Mendoza

When I Fall In Love • SSAA 259
Victor Young, arranged by Kirby Shaw

Glossary 269

Classified Index 285

Index of Songs and Spotlights 287

TO THE STUDENT

Welcome to choir!

By singing in the choir, you have chosen to be a part of an exciting and rewarding adventure. The benefits of being in choir are many. Basically, singing is fun. It provides an expressive way of sharing your feelings and emotions. Through choir, you will have friends that share a common interest with you. You will experience the joy of making beautiful music together. Choir provides the opportunity to develop your interpersonal skills. It takes teamwork and cooperation to sing together, and you must learn how to work with others. As you critique your individual and group performances, you can improve your ability to analyze and communicate your thoughts clearly.

Even if you do not pursue a music career, music can be an important part of your life. There are many avocational opportunities in music. **Avocational** means *not related to a job or career*. Singing as a hobby can provide you with personal enjoyment, enrich your life, and teach you life skills. Singing is something you can do for the rest of your life.

In this course, you will be presented with the basic skills of vocal production and music literacy. You will be exposed to songs from different cultures, songs in many different styles and languages, and songs from various historical periods. You will discover connections between music and the other arts. Guidelines for becoming a better singer and choir member include:

- Come to class prepared to learn.
- Respect the efforts of others.
- Work daily to improve your sight-singing skills.
- Sing expressively at all times.
- Have fun singing.

This book was written to provide you with a meaningful choral experience. Take advantage of the knowledge and opportunities offered here. Your exciting adventure of experiencing choral music is about to begin!

Lessons

Lessons for the Beginning of the Year

1   In Time Of Silver Rain 2

2   Shiru 10

3   Didn't My Lord Deliver Daniel 20

4   The Star-Spangled Banner 32

Lessons for Mid-Winter

5   Homeland 36

6   Domine Fili Unigenite 48

7   Through Winter's Window 56

8   Go Where I Send Thee! 66

Lessons for Concert/Festival

9   Vere languores nostros 76

10   Overture To *Die Zauberflöte* 82

11   Die Schwestern 94

12   Fire 104

In Time Of Silver Rain

Composer: Audrey Snyder
Text: Langston Hughes
Voicing: SSA

 SPOTLIGHT

To learn more about breath management, see page 9.

VOCABULARY

minor tonality

canon

imitation

word painting

Focus

- Read and perform music in the key of G minor.
- Describe and perform imitation in music.
- Explain the relationship between music and poetry.

Getting Started

Take a moment and look around your classroom. Describe what you see in this room and how that is different from other classrooms. Observations such as these help us become more aware of the world in which we live. The African American poet Langston Hughes (1902–1967) might have stopped on a beautiful spring day and observed his surroundings. Hughes describes the loveliness of spring in his poem "In Time Of Silver Rain." Read the text of this song and find ways in which Hughes has skillfully articulated what he has observed.

◆ History and Culture

Langston Hughes is regarded as one of America's greatest poets. In addition to poetry, he wrote novels, short stories and plays. His writings are colorful and insightful portrayals of African American life during the twentieth century. His interest in jazz is evident in the rhythmical language of his poetry. As a result, many of his poems have been set to music.

Composer Audrey Snyder is quoted as saying, "I loved the poem from the first moment I read it because it so simply and perfectly captured the essence of springtime when the world wakes from winter and new life emerges. Through his words, Langston Hughes has recreated the feelings of renewal that I have when I venture outside after a long, cold winter."

Links to Learning

◆ Vocal

"In Time Of Silver Rain" begins in the key of G minor and is based on the G minor scale. *A song that is based on a minor scale with* la *as its keynote, or home tone, is described* as being in **minor tonality**. Sing the G minor scale. Then, sing the scale again in a canon with the second group starting as indicated. A **canon** is *a musical form in which one part sings a melody, and the other parts sing the same melody, but enter at different times.*

G	A	B♭	C	D	E♭	F	G	F	E♭	D	C	B♭	A	G
la	ti	do	re	mi	fa	sol	la	sol	fa	mi	re	do	ti	la

◆ Theory

Imitation is *the act of one part copying what another has already sung.* Perform the example below to practice singing imitation between parts.

◆ Artistic Expression

Composers sometimes use **word painting** *(a technique in which the music reflects the meaning of the words)* in their writing to link the text to the music. In this piece, examples of word painting include "catch a rainbow cry" (melody outlines the arch of a rainbow) and "wonder spreads" (repeated numerous times to indicate spreading out). Find these examples in the music.

Evaluation

Demonstrate how well you have learned the skills and concepts featured in the lesson "In Time Of Silver Rain" by completing the following:

- With a partner, sing the G minor scale in unison and then again in a canon to show you can sing in minor tonality. How well did you do?

- Identify other musical passages in which the composer uses word painting. How can this technique enhance a piece of music?

This arrangement for The Frederick Children's Choir Tenth Anniversary, Judith Du Bose, Director

In Time Of Silver Rain

For SSA and Piano

**Text by
LANGSTON HUGHES**

**Music by
AUDREY SNYDER**

SPOTLIGHT

Posture & Breath Management

There are some basic techniques to help you sing higher, lower, louder, softer and for longer periods of time without tiring. First, a singer needs to have proper posture. Try the following exercise:

1. Stand with your feet shoulder width apart and knees unlocked.
2. Balance your head effortlessly on the top of your spine.
3. Exhale all of your air.
4. Raise your arms up over your head.
5. Take in a deep breath as if you were sipping through a straw.
6. Slowly lower your arms down to your sides.
7. Let out your air on a breathy "pah" without letting your chest drop.

Now that you have discovered proper posture, try this for discovering how a singer should breathe and manage the breath:

1. Place your hands on your waist at the bottom of your ribcage.
2. Take in an easy breath without lifting your chest or shoulders.
3. Feel your waist and ribcage expand all the way around like an inflating inner tube.
4. Let your breath out slowly on "sss," feeling your inner tube deflating as if it has a slow leak.
5. Remember to keep your chest up the entire time.
6. Take in another easy breath over four counts before your inner tube has completely deflated, then let your air out on "sss" for eight counts.
7. Repeat this step several times, taking in an easy breath over four counts and gradually increasing the number of release counts to sixteen.
8. Once you have reached sixteen counts, try to see how many times you can repeat it without getting tired.

Practice this every day, gradually working up to five minutes of repetition. If you become lightheaded, you are taking in too much air for the number of counts you are exhaling.

A "catch breath," which is required when you don't have much time to breathe, should feel like the kind of breath you take when you are pleasantly surprised or see something lovely for the first time. It must be silent, though!

Shiru

Composer: Allan E. Naplan
Text: Psalms 96 and 98 (adapted)
Voicing: 2-Part

VOCABULARY
psalm
scale
major scale
syncopation

Focus

- Read, write and perform music in the key of G major.
- Read and perform rhythmic patterns that contain syncopation.
- Perform music in a foreign language.

Getting Started

You come to choir class to sing, but you don't always get to sing in English. Here is the term "we sing" in five different languages. Can you identify the languages?

> *nous chantons*
> *Wir singen*
> *cantemos*
> *cantiamo*
> *shiru*

"Shiru," the Hebrew word for "we sing," is the title that composer Allan Naplan chose for this spirited song of celebration. The captivating rhythms and simple melody in this song will make the Hebrew text easy to learn.

◆ **History and Culture**

"Shiru" is based on Psalms 96 and 98. A **psalm** is *a song, lyric poem, or prayer that is found in the Old Testament of the Bible.* The psalms have been set to music for centuries and can be found in almost every style of music. The English translation is:

> *Sing a new song. Sing, shout all the earth.*
> *Break forth, sing aloud, and play music.*
> *Shout all the earth. Sing all the earth. Sing a new song.*
> *Let the heavens rejoice. Let the earth be glad.*
> *Let the sea roar, and all that fills it.*
> *Let the field exult, and all that is in it.*
> *Let the trees of the forest sing for joy.*
> *Let the rivers clap hands. Let the mountain sing for joy.*
> *Sing a new song. Sing, shout all the earth.*
> *Sing a new song. SING!*

SKILL BUILDERS

To learn more about the key of G major, see Proficient Sight-Singing, *page 71.*

Links to Learning

◆ Vocal

This song begins in the key of G major and is based on the G major scale. A **scale** is *a group of notes that are sung in succession and are based on a particular home tone, or keynote*. A **major scale** is *the scale that has* do *as its keynote, or home tone*. To locate "G" on the piano, find any set of three black keys. "G" is the white key just to the left of the middle black key. This scale uses the notes G, A, B, C, D, E, F♯, G. Using the keyboard below as a guide, play the G major scale.

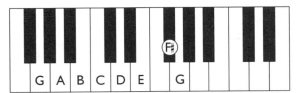

Sing the G major scale.

G	A	B	C	D	E	F♯	G	F♯	E	D	C	B	A	G
do	re	mi	fa	sol	la	ti	do	ti	la	sol	fa	mi	re	do

◆ Theory

Excitement and energy are generated by the rhythmic drive of this piece. The rhythms contain **syncopation,** *the placement of accents on a weak beat or the weak portion of the beat*. Read and perform the following syncopated rhythms. Find these examples in the music.

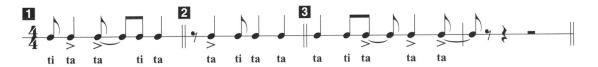

Evaluation

Demonstrate how well you have learned the skills and concepts featured in the lesson "Shiru" by completing the following:

- Write a four-measure melody in the key of G major. Begin and end your melody on *do*. Check your work for rhythmic and melodic accuracy.

- Chant or clap the rhythms in measures 47–55 to show your ability to read and perform syncopated rhythms. Rate your performance on a scale of 1 to 5, with 5 being the best.

Commissioned by the Haddonfield Festival Chorus, Haddonfield, New Jersey
Polly Murray and Ellen Phillips, Directors

Shiru
(Sing)

For 2-Part and Piano

Text adapted from
Psalms 96 and 98

Music by
ALLAN E. NAPLAN

Didn't My Lord Deliver Daniel

Composer: Traditional Spiritual, arranged by Ken Berg
Text: Traditional
Voicing: SSA

VOCABULARY

spiritual

diction

melodic minor scale

syncopation

SPOTLIGHT

To learn more about vocal health, see page 185.

Focus

• Perform music in minor tonality.

• Demonstrate musical artistry through expression and proper diction.

• Perform music representing the African American spiritual.

Getting Started

go team

Go Team

GO TEAM!

Words can have power. When a statement is repeated over and over with energy and emotion, it can gain momentum. Think of a statement and speak it out loud three times, increasing the emphasis and energy each time. Ken Berg uses this technique in "Didn't My Lord Deliver Daniel" to emphasize the words "didn't my Lord" at the beginning of the spiritual and again in the middle of the piece. Be sure to sing each repetition of these words with increased energy, support and momentum.

◆ History and Culture

"Didn't My Lord Deliver Daniel" is a **spiritual,** or *a song that was first sung by African American slaves.* Spirituals are usually based on biblical themes or stories. These songs were probably sung while the slaves were working in the fields, engaging in social activities, or participating in worship. Syncopation and complex rhythms are often found in spirituals.

When performing "Didn't My Lord Deliver Daniel," pay special attention to the **diction,** or *the pronunciation of the words while singing,* so that you can be clearly understood. Be careful not to stress the final consonants of words, and sing this song with energy and enthusiasm.

Links to Learning

◆ **Vocal**

This piece begins in the key of D minor and is based on the D melodic minor scale. A **melodic minor scale** is *a minor scale that uses raised sixth and seventh notes*, fi *(raised from* fa) *and* si *(raised from* sol). Often, these notes are raised in ascending patterns, but not in descending patterns. Read and perform the following examples to practice the D melodic minor scale and the interval skips found in the scale.

◆ **Theory**

Syncopation is *the placement of accents on a weak beat or a weak portion of the beat*. Perform the following example to practice syncopation. Find these patterns in the music.

◆ **Artistic Expression**

Chant the text in measures 9–24. As each phrase is repeated, increase the momentum and energy level. This technique will add artistic expression to your performance.

Evaluation

Demonstrate how well you have learned the skills and concepts featured in the lesson "Didn't My Lord Deliver Daniel" by completing the following:

• Sing measures 9–16 to show your ability to sing with accurate intonation in minor tonality. Evaluate yourself on how well you did.

• Listen to a rehearsal or performance recording of "Didn't My Lord Deliver Daniel." Draw a diagram that represents the ensemble's energy level during the chorus of the song (measures 17–33, 48–56, 72–89). In what ways did the energy level change?

For the Birmingham Boys Choir, Susan Berg, Pianist

Didn't My Lord Deliver Daniel

For SSA and Piano

Arranged by
KEN BERG

Traditional Spiritual

my Lord de-liv-er Dan - iel,__ then __ why not ev - 'ry man?__

my Lord de-liv-er Dan - iel,__ then __ why not ev - 'ry man?__

He de - liv-er'd Dan - iel from the li-on's den,__

He de - liv-er'd Dan - iel from the li-on's den,__

Jo-nah from the bel - ly of the whale,_____ and the He-brew chil - dren from the

Jo-nah from the bel - ly of the whale,_____ and the He-brew chil - dren from the

Dan - iel, ___ de - liv - er D - D - D - D - Dan - iel, did - n't my Lord de - liv - er

Dan - iel, ___ de - liv - er D - D - D - D - Dan - iel, did - n't my Lord de - liv - er

75

Dan - iel, ___ then ___ why not ev - 'ry man, ___ then ___

Dan - iel, ___ then ___ why not ev - 'ry man, ___ then ___

subito p

78

why not ev - 'ry man, ___ then ___ why not

why not ev - 'ry man, ___ then ___ why not

subito ff

81

The Star-Spangled Banner

Composer: John Stafford Smith (1759–1836), arranged by Barry Talley
Text: Francis Scott Key
Voicing: SSAA

VOCABULARY

national anthem

accidental

SPOTLIGHT

To learn more about concert etiquette, see page 114.

Focus

- Describe and sing accidentals accurately.
- Read and perform rhythmic patterns that contain dotted rhythms.
- Relate the music to history, to society and to culture.

Getting Started

The flag and the **national anthem** *(a patriotic song adopted by a nation through tradition or decree)* are symbols of national pride and patriotism. What does the phrase "O'er the land of the free and the home of the brave" mean to you? What images do you visualize when you sing "The Star-Spangled Banner"? Write down your thoughts and share them with the class.

◆ History and Culture

You may know who wrote the words to "The Star-Spangled Banner," but do you know who wrote the original music? His name is John Stafford Smith (1759–1836). Smith was an English composer and organist who composed "To Anachreon in Heaven" in 1770 for the London Anacreonic Society, an aristocratic group dedicated to the promotion of the arts. Later, the words, written by Francis Scott Key, were set to this tune.

During the War of 1812, the British fleet attacked Fort McHenry, which is located outside Baltimore, Maryland. During the attack, Francis Scott Key was aboard a British warship trying to gain the release of an American prisoner. The next morning, the flag, though battered and torn, was still there. Inspired by this sight, Key wrote the words to "The Star-Spangled Banner" on the back of a letter he had in his pocket. It was printed on flyers the next day and distributed throughout Baltimore. In 1931, the United States Congress officially recognized "The Star-Spangled Banner" as our national anthem.

Links to Learning

◆ **Vocal**

Although this arrangement is written in the key of C major, it uses **accidentals** *(any sharp, flat or natural that is not included in the key signature of a piece of music)* to change the pitch of some notes. The pitch *fa* is sometimes raised to *fi*, and the pitch *sol* is sometimes raised to *si*. Perform the following C major scale with accidentals.

do   re   mi   fa   fi   sol   si   la   ti   do   ti   la   si   sol   fi   fa   mi   re   do

For more practice singing accidentals, perform the following example.

do   re   mi   fa   sol   la   ti   do   do   do   ti   la   sol   fa   mi   re   do   do

do   re   mi   fi   sol   si   la   ti   do   do   ti   la   si   sol   fi   fa   mi   re   do   do

◆ **Theory**

Read and perform the following rhythmic patterns that contain dotted rhythms.

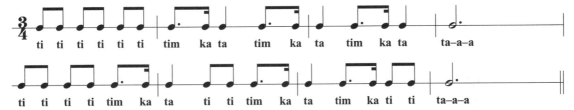

ti ti ti ti ti ti   tim ka ta   tim ka ta   tim ka ta   ta–a–a

ti ti ti ti tim ka ta   ti ti tim ka ta   tim ka ti ti   ta–a–a

Evaluation

Demonstrate how well you have learned the skills and concepts featured in the lesson "The Star-Spangled Banner" by completing the following:

- Sing the Vocal examples above to show your ability to sing altered pitches in tune. You may do this with a partner taking turns singing for each other. Critique each other's performance.

- Chant or clap the rhythms in measures 5–13 that contain dotted notes. Rate how well you were able to perform the rhythms: (1) all rhythms were correct, (2) most rhythms were correct, (3) only a few rhythms were correct.

For the 1999 Texas All-State Choir
The Star-Spangled Banner
For SSAA, a cappella

Arranged by
BARRY TALLEY

Words by FRANCIS SCOTT KEY
Music by JOHN STAFFORD SMITH (1759–1836)

Homeland

Composer: Gustav Holst (1874–1934), arranged by Z. Randall Stroope
Text: Sir Cecil Spring-Rice (1859–1918) and Z. Randall Stroope
Voicing: SSA

VOCABULARY

ABA form

coda

interval

$\frac{3}{4}$ meter

Focus

- Describe and demonstrate an understanding of ABA form.
- Interpret the meaning of the text through the performance of the music.
- Perform patriotic music.

Getting Started

The ceremonies and celebrations in Great Britain are noteworthy for stirring music and much pomp and circumstance. For instance, if you were to attend the following British events, you might hear these beloved songs:

Event	Song
State Opening of Parliament	"Land of Hope and Glory"
Trooping the Colour (the Queen's birthday)	"God Save the Queen"
Royal Navy ceremony	"Rule Britannia!"

And if you were to attend a British school assembly, you might hear the students singing "I Vow to Thee, My Country." American composer Z. Randall Stroope used this British favorite to begin "Homeland."

 **SKILL BUILDERS**

To learn more about $\frac{3}{4}$ meter, see Proficient Sight-Singing, *page 14.*

◆ History and Culture

Z. Randall Stroope chose the first verse of "I Vow to Thee, My Country" by Sir Cecil Spring-Rice (1859–1918) as the text for "Homeland." Since 1918, this text has been sung to a melody from "Jupiter," the Fourth Movement of *The Planets*, an orchestral suite by British composer Gustav Holst (1874–1934).

Stroope uses ABA form and coda to give "Homeland" strength and unity. **ABA form** is *the design in which the opening phrases (section A) are followed by contrasting phrases (section B), which leads to a repetition of the opening phrases (section A).* The **coda** is *a special ending to a song.* Find these sections in the music. How does the return of section A differ from the opening?

Links to Learning

◆ **Vocal**

Read and perform the following example to practice the intervals found in "Homeland." An **interval** is *the distance between two different notes.*

do mi sol la do ti sol do re do ti do____

To prepare to sing the harmonies used in this piece, perform the following example.

Loo, loo, loo, loo, loo, loo, loo, loo, loo._____

◆ **Theory**

Read and perform the following rhythmic patterns in ¾ **meter,** *a time signature in which there are three beats per measure and the quarter note receives the beat.*

ti ti tam ti tim ka ti ti ta ta ti ti ta ta tam

◆ **Artistic Expression**

The instructions at measure 13 are to sing "with enduring strength." In your opinion, what does this mean as it relates to the performance of this patriotic song? Study the text and express its powerful meaning as you perform.

Evaluation

Demonstrate how well you have learned the skills and concepts featured in the lesson "Homeland" by completing the following:

- Using the medium of visual arts, create a simple sketch, painting or sculpture that represents ABA form to show your understanding of this form.

- In your own words, write a brief summary of the meaning of the text in verse 1 (measures 13–37), verse 2 (measures 41–62), and verse 3 (measures 68–93). How can a better understanding of the words improve your performance?

Commissioned for the Council Bluffs, Iowa,
All-School Festival

Homeland

For SSA and Piano

Arranged by Z. RANDALL STROOPE
Additional words by Z. RANDALL STROOPE

Words by SIR CECIL SPRING-RICE (1859–1918)
Music by GUSTAV HOLST (1874–1934)

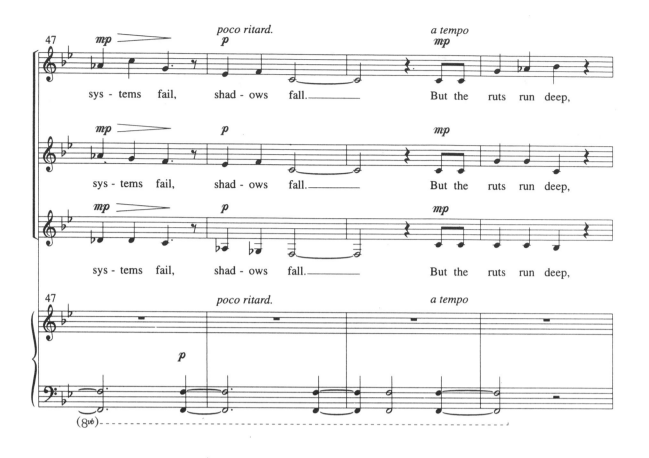

sys - tems fail, shad - ows fall._____ But the ruts run deep,

sys - tems fail, shad - ows fall._____ But the ruts run deep,

sys - tems fail, shad - ows fall._____ But the ruts run deep,

cut by the blood of fac - es a - bove, And voic - es now

cut by the blood of fac - es a - bove, And voic - es now

cut by the blood of fac - es a - bove, And voic - es now

sword; May your strength be forged with mer - cy, your cour - age lives* re -

sword; May your strength be forged with mer - cy, your cour - age lives* re -

poco ritard.
unis.

store. Home - land, the coun - try that I love, for - ev - er reign su -

store. Home - land, the coun - try that I love, for - ev - er reign su -

poco ritard.

div. *ff*

preme; And when time stands still, my home - land, may heav - en hold your

ff

preme; And when time stands still, my home - land, may heav - en hold your

ff

* plural of "life"

Domine Fili Unigenite

Composer: Giovanni Pierluigi da Palestrina (1525–1594), edited by Matthew Michaels
Text: Liturgical Latin
Voicing: SSA

VOCABULARY

Renaissance period
Gregorian chant
polyphony
melisma
cut time

MUSIC & HISTORY

To learn more about the Renaissance period, see page 116.

Focus

• Describe and perform music from the Renaissance period.

• Sing melismas correctly.

• Perform rhythmic patterns in cut time.

Getting Started

Have you ever worn your hair in braids? If so, you know that you must first divide your hair into three equal parts. Then, if you work the braid evenly, it will be neat and hang straight. You will look awesome. This setting of "Domine Fili Unigenite" by Palestrina could be considered a musical braid. It is divided into three equal parts that musically weave together to make a complete composition. When all three parts can be sung with independence, you will sound awesome.

◆ History and Culture

Composer Giovanni Pierluigi da Palestrina (1525–1594) lived and worked during the **Renaissance period** (*c. 1430–1600*) of Western music history. He served as a choirmaster and organist in Rome, Italy, during most of his life. The greatest part of his writing was in the area of sacred music, including 104 masses, 250 motets and many other liturgical compositions.

Before the Renaissance period, a significant vocal form was the **Gregorian chant,** *a single unaccompanied melodic line sung by male voices.* As this style developed, additional melodic lines were added. This was the beginning of **polyphony,** *a type of music in which two or more different melodic lines are sung at the same time.* Polyphonic music was refined during the Renaissance, and this period is sometimes called the "golden age of polyphony." Palestrina is considered the master of polyphonic music, and his "Domine Fili Unigenite" is an excellent example.

Links to Learning

◆ Vocal

A **melisma** is *many notes that are sung on one syllable or word*. Sing the following example on solfège syllables. Then, sing it again on the neutral syllable "doo." Continue until every note is sung distinctly, yet connected with your breath. Finally, sing with the text. Start slowly, and then gradually increase to the performance tempo.

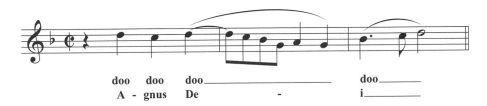

doo   doo   doo_____   doo_____
A - gnus   De   -   i_____

◆ Theory

Chant, tap or clap the following rhythmic pattern that is written in **cut time** *(a time signature in which there are two beats per measure and the half note receives the beat)*. Conduct a two-beat pattern as you chant the rhythm.

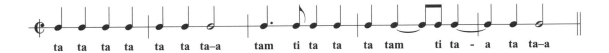

ta   ta   ta   ta   ta   ta   ta–a   tam   ti   ta   ta   ta   tam   ti   ta - a   ta   ta–a

Evaluation

Demonstrate how well you have learned the skills and concepts featured in the lesson "Domine Fili Unigenite" by completing the following:

• Discuss the musical characteristics of the Renaissance period.

• Sing measures 22–34 to show that you can sing melismas with a light tone. Evaluate the quality of your vocal tone.

• In a trio (three singers) with one singer per part, sing measures 1–22 to show your ability to read and perform music in cut time. Identify which measures need improvement.

Domine Fili Unigenite

(from MISSA PRIMI TONI)

For SSA a cappella

Edited by MATTHEW MICHAELS

GIOVANNI PIERLUIGI da PALESTRINA
(1525–1594)

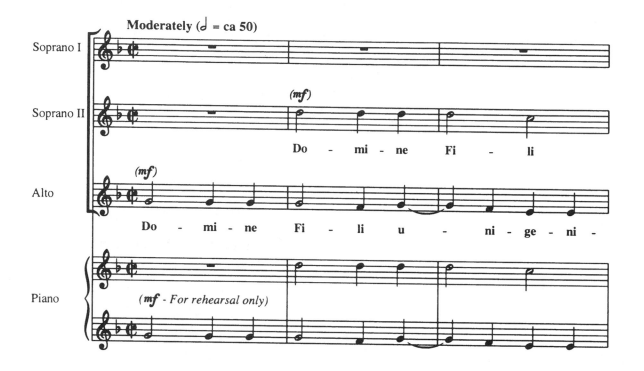

Through Winter's Window

Composer: Brad Printz
Text: Ann and Brad Printz
Voicing: SSA

VOCABULARY

syllabic stress

dot

SKILL BUILDERS

To learn more about dotted rhythms, see Proficient Sight-Singing, *page 76.*

Focus

- Identify and perform dotted rhythms.
- Use visual art techniques to interpret musical content and style.

Getting Started

Go in and out the window, Go in and out the window,

Go in and out the window As we have done before.

Do you know the tune to this old American folk song? Did you sing it when you were young? Where is your favorite window in your house? Have you gazed out that window enough times that you could describe the view from memory? If the window were a picture frame, could you draw the view? Ann and Brad Printz's view in "Through Winter's Window" is a sharp, crisp and still winter's night that compels us to be appreciative for such a peaceful and joyful scene.

◆ History and Culture

The text of "Through Winter's Window" paints a visual image with words. If the words are sung rather than spoken, the composer becomes the paintbrush and can choose melodies for colors, harmonies for texture, and rhythms for form. You and your choir are the canvas. You decide how the song will be presented. Here are some questions to think about:

1. How long are the phrases? How will you manage your breath support?

2. What dynamic and expressive markings need to be observed?

3. What can you do to ensure that all three vocal lines are blended and balanced?

Links to Learning

◆ Vocal

Practice singing the following words three different ways: 1) with equal stress on syllables one and two, 2) with stress only on syllable one, and 3) with stress only on syllable two. Which interpretation best fits the musical phrases of this piece, as well as the natural spoken text? Singers refer to this as **syllabic stress,** or *the placement of stress on one syllable over another.*

peace - ful   eve - ning   sun - set

◆ Theory

A **dot** is *a symbol that increases the length of a given note by half its value.* It is placed to the right of the note. The following example includes a dotted eighth note and a dotted quarter note. Perform the rhythms in the following example.

tim ka tam   ti ka ti ti   tam   ti ta–a

◆ Artistic Expression

Choose from the piece a phrase of text that describes a winter evening. Use drawing, painting or any form of three-dimensional art to create a window scene. Use elements of your visual image to decide on a musical interpretation for your chosen phrase.

Evaluation

Demonstrate how well you have learned the skills and concepts featured in the lesson "Through Winter's Window" by completing the following:

- Write a four-measure rhythm phrase in $\frac{4}{4}$ meter that includes dotted eighth and dotted quarter notes. Exchange your phrase with a classmate and perform them for one another. Critique each other's work.

- With a small group, arrange your artwork windows in song order so you can sing while following your "art score." Choose expressive and dynamic interpretations that match the images of the art score. Perform your interpretation for the class. How does the artwork add to your performance?

Through Winter's Window

For SSA and Piano

Words by ANN PRINTZ
and BRAD PRINTZ

Music by BRAD PRINTZ

* alternate text "Christmas"

SPOTLIGHT

Physiology Of The Voice

Physiology is a branch of biology that deals with living organisms and their parts. It is interesting to see how the parts of the human body work together to produce vocal sound. Vocal production requires the following elements:

The Actuators

The actuators are parts of the body involved in the breathing process. The parts of the airway include (1) head airways (the nose and mouth), (2) pharynx (throat tube), (3) larynx (voice box), (4) trachea (windpipe), (5) bronchi (two branches of trachea that lead into the lungs), and (6) lungs. The muscles used in breathing include (1) the abdominals (belly muscles), (2) intercostals (muscles attached to the ribs), and (3) diaphragm (a horizontal, dome-shaped muscle separating the chest and abdominal cavities).

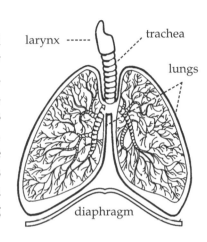

The Vibrators

The vocal folds (or "vocal cords") are housed in the larynx (the voice box) at the top of the trachea and vibrate when air from the lungs passes between them.

The Resonators

The sound waves produced by the vocal folds are enhanced and amplified by the resonators or natural cavities located in the pharynx, larynx, mouth, nasal passages and sinus passages.

The Articulators

The articulators are the parts of the body used in speech, namely the lips, teeth, tongue, jaw and soft palate. To find the soft palate, place the tip of your tongue on the roof of your mouth and slide it toward your throat just past the bony ridge of your hard palate.

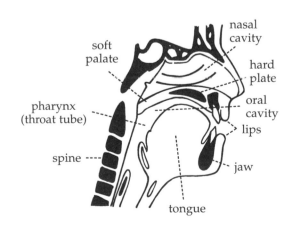

Go Where I Send Thee!

Composer: Gospel Spiritual, arranged by Paul Caldwell and Sean Ivory
Text: Traditional Spiritual
Voicing: SSA

VOCABULARY

cumulative song

gospel music

chromatic scale

Focus

- Read and perform chromatic passages accurately.

- Demonstrate the ability to read and perform syncopated rhythms.

- Perform music representing gospel music.

 SPOTLIGHT

To learn more about gospel music, see page 75.

Getting Started

"The Twelve Days of Christmas"

"Rattlin' Bog"

"I Know An Old Lady Who Swallowed A Fly"

Do you know these traditional songs? Can you sing them? Do they have anything in common? Here are some hints:

a. All of the songs have many verses.

b. You will have the first verse memorized in no time.

These songs are all cumulative songs. A **cumulative song** is *a song form in which each time a verse is sung, more words are added.* These songs are exceptionally fun to sing. The song you are about to learn, "Go Where I Send Thee!" is a great example of a cumulative song.

◆ History and Culture

"Go Where I Send Thee!" is an example of African American **gospel music,** *a type of religious music that originated in the African American churches of the South and is characterized by improvisation, syncopation and repetition.* The numbers in this cumulative song give the singers one-line reminders of certain personalities and stories from the Bible. For example, "eight" refers to the number of people instructed to board Noah's ark: Noah, his wife, his three sons and their wives. The number "three" represents the three Hebrew children: Shadrach, Meshach and Abednego.

Links to Learning

◆ Vocal

The **chromatic scale** is *a scale that consists of all half steps and uses all twelve pitches in an octave.* Read and perform the following chromatic scale.

C C♯ D D♯ E F F♯ G G♯ A A♯ B C B B♭ A A♭ G G♭ F E E♭ D D♭ C

do di re ri mi fa fi sol si la li ti do ti te la le sol se fa mi ma re ra do

Perform the following example to practice singing chords that move chromatically.

Soprano I

Dah, dah, dah, dah, dah, dah, dah, dah, dah, dah, dah.

Soprano II

Dah, dah, dah, dah, dah, dah, dah, dah, dah, dah, dah.

Alto

Dah, dah, dah, dah, dah, dah, dah, dah, dah, dah, dah.

◆ Theory

To perform the following example, clap on the down beat (C) and turn your right hand over and brush it across the palm of your left hand on the up beat (B). Chant the words as you clap and brush the steady eighth note pulse. Then, divide into three groups and perform as a three-part canon one beat apart as indicated.

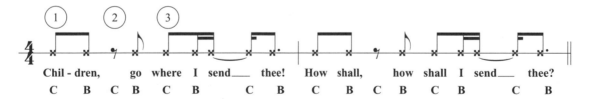

Chil - dren, go where I send___ thee! How shall, how shall I send___ thee?
C B C B C B C B C B C B C B C B

Evaluation

Demonstrate how well you have learned the skills and concepts featured in the lesson "Go Where I Send Thee!" by completing the following:

- In a trio with one singer on a part, sing the chromatic chord progression found in the Vocal section above. Evaluate how well you were able to sing the half steps in tune.

- Sing measures 47–48 to show you can perform syncopated rhythms accurately. How well did you do?

Go Where I Send Thee!

For SSA and Piano

**Arranged by
PAUL CALDWELL and SEAN IVORY**

Gospel Spiritual

how shall I send __ thee?   I'm gon-na send thee six __ by six, __

six for the days when the world was fixed, __   five for the bread they did __ di - vide, __

four for the Gos - pel writ - ers, __   three for the He - brew chil - dren, __

two for Paul and Si - las, __   one for the lit - tle bit - ty ba - by, __ the

(loco)

SPOTLIGHT

Gospel Music

Gospel music is *religious music that originated in the African American churches of the South*. Characteristics of gospel music include improvisation, syncopation and repetition. Following the Civil War, African American churches began to emerge. The spirituals sung by the early slaves served as their main source of sacred music. By the early 1900s, some sectors of the church moved to more spirited songs accompanied by tambourines, drums and piano. These were the earliest versions of gospel music.

African American gospel music gained national recognition during the 1940s and the 1950s with the recordings and live concerts by the singing great Mahalia Jackson. Also influential was Thomas Andrew Dorsey (1899–1993). He published over 400 gospel songs and is known as the father of gospel music. His gospel music used lively rhythms and syncopated piano accompaniments. "Precious Lord, Take My Hand" is probably his most famous song.

When asked about the correct way to sing gospel music, contemporary composer Rollo Dilworth shared these thoughts. He said that singers often debate about the appropriate use of chest voice and head voice registers when performing gospel style. While some believe that excessive use of the chest voice might cause vocal damage, others believe that singing in the African American idiom is not "authentic" if performed in head voice. Dilworth suggests that successful singing in most any genre requires a balanced, healthy singing tone in both head and chest registers.

Vocal techniques used in gospel singing include (1) percussive singing (a style that lies between legato and staccato styles); (2) swell (an exaggerated crescendo that adds weight and breadth to an accented syllable); and (3) pitch bending (or the scooping up to a pitch, often coupled with a swell or that "falling off" of a pitch). The rhythm is felt in an accurate yet relaxed style. Basic movements may include stepping, clapping and rocking. Improvisation of melody is frequently heard in gospel music.

Listen to a recording of "Go Where I Send Thee" on page 66 and identify characteristics of gospel-style singing.

Vere Languores Nostros

Composer: Antonio Lotti (1667–1740)
Text: Latin Sacred
Voicing: SSA

VOCABULARY

Baroque period

minor chord

major chord

messa di voce

Focus

• Describe and perform music from the Baroque period.

• Identify aurally and by notation major and minor chords.

MUSIC & HISTORY

*To learn more about the
Baroque period,
see page 120.*

Getting Started

For centuries, young people have been drawn together as a community through their love of music. Whether singing or listening, the music we share can give us a sense of belonging to a group, sharing our common values, and exploring new ideas through our repertoire. How did the youth music movement of the 1920s and again in the 1950s and 1960s change society? In what ways does the music that you and your friends listen to influence your community of friends at large?

◆ History and Culture

Antonio Lotti (1667–1740) lived during the **Baroque period** *(1600–1750)*. Although born and raised in Hanover, Germany, Lotti spent most of his adult life between Germany and Venice, Italy. He was a senior musician with the Basilica of St. Marks in Venice. In addition, he wrote music for a girls' choir associated with the local school and orphanage called Ospedale degli Incuradili. "Vere Languores Nostros" was written for that school. Music making became so important at the school that Venetian noblemen would place their daughters' names on waiting lists to gain admittance.

The Baroque period witnessed the rise of humanism and a belief of "moving the emotions." A characteristic of music of this period is that a single composition or movement tended to project a single mood or expression of feeling. What mood is expressed in "Vere Languores Nostros?"

Links to Learning

◆ **Theory**

A **minor chord** is *a chord that is built on the intervals of a minor third and a major third.* In "Vere Languores Nostros," you will find the F minor chord using the pitches *la, do* and *mi.* Sing the F minor chord.

A **major chord** is *a chord that is built on the intervals of a major third and a minor third.* In this song, you will find the C major chord using the pitches *mi, si* and *ti.* Sing the C major chord.

Play the following chords on a piano or keyboard, and determine by listening which are major chords and which are minor chords.

◆ **Artistic Expression**

Messa di voce, or *a technique of singing a slight crescendo and decrescendo on a held note,* was common in music of the Baroque period. Find the musical marking for *messa di voce* in measure 1 of "Vere Languores Nostros." Prepare a list of all dynamic markings found in this piece. Discuss how the use of dynamics can add expression to your performance.

Evaluation

Demonstrate how well you have learned the skills and concepts featured in the lesson "Vere Languores Nostros" by completing the following:

- Look in your music and identify the chords found in measures 1, 4 (second half of beat) and 5 as major or minor chords. How well did you do?

- In a trio with one on a part, sing measures 1–22. Rate your performance based on 1) singing with accurate intonation, 2) the use of effective dynamics, and 3) singing with correct phrasing.

Vere Languores Nostros

For SSA, a cappella

Edited by
THOMAS JUNEAU

ANTONIO LOTTI (1667–1740)

80 Proficient Treble

Overture to *Die Zauberflöte*

Composer: Wolfgang Amadeus Mozart (1756–1791), arranged by Arkadi Serper
Text: Arkadi Serper
Voicing: SSAA

VOCABULARY
Classical period
overture
motive

MUSIC & HISTORY

To learn more about the Classical period, see page 124.

Focus

- Describe and perform music from the Classical period.
- Explore unconventional choral-ensemble tone color.
- Improvise a text using neutral syllables.

Getting Started

Take a poll in your choir and find out how many singers play a band or orchestra instrument. Make a list of the represented instruments. Singers who are also instrumentalists have a wonderful perspective for comparing and contrasting choral and instrumental music. Besides the obvious element of a text, can you think of other differences between instrumental and choral music? Are there more similarities or differences?

◆ History and Culture

In 1963 a small group of singers directed by Ward Swingle decided to explore these differences by using their voices like instruments. Swingle began by arranging familiar instrumental pieces by Johann Sebastian Bach (1685–1750) for mixed ensembles. The instrumental lines were sung on neutral syllables. The Swingle Singers' music became instantly popular. This arrangement of Wolfgang Amadeus Mozart's (1756–1791) "Overture to *Die Zauberflöte*" is reminiscent of the Swingle Singers.

Mozart is perhaps one of the most famous composers in Western music. He lived in Vienna, Austria, and worked as a professional musician during the **Classical period** *(1750–1820)*. He began composing music at the age of five. Among Mozart's many compositions were symphonies, operas, cantatas, oratorios, chamber music, sonatas, concertos and more. His masterful opera *Die Zauberflöte* ("The Magic Flute") is filled with glorious vocal music. This vivacious arrangement of the **overture** *(an instrumental piece that serves as an introduction to an opera or other dramatic work)* gives your choir the opportunity to vocally experience Mozart's instrumental brilliance.

Links to Learning

◆ Theory

Mozart uses a rhythmic **motive** (*a short rhythmic or melodic idea that is repeated throughout a piece of music*) throughout the overture. Perform the following example by chanting the syllables while maintaining a steady beat. How many times does this rhythmic motive appear in your voice part?

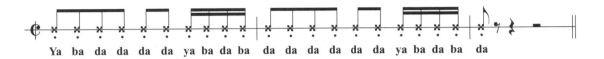

Ya ba da da da da ya ba da ba   da da da da da da ya ba da ba   da

◆ Artistic Expression

Use the library or the Internet to research the opera *Die Zauberflöte*. Make a list of the characters in the opera and what voice part they sing. Write a short plot summary of the story. In what ways will this information help you interpret the music as you sing the "Overture to *Die Zauberflöte*"?

Evaluation

Demonstrate how well you have learned the skills and concepts featured in the lesson "Overture to *Die Zauberflöte*" by completing the following:

- Find four appearances of the principal rhythmic motive (as presented in the Vocal section above) in your voice part. Sing one of the rhythmic motives for a classmate using solfège syllables. How accurately did you sing the rhythms?

- Choose a favorite four-measure phrase from your voice part. Improvise a new set of neutral syllables to enhance the style of the phrase. Share your improvisation with another member of the class. How were your improvisations similar? In what ways were they different?

Overture To *Die Zauberflöte*

SSAA, a cappella

Vocal Arrangement by ARKADI SERPER

WOLFGANG AMADEUS MOZART (1756–1791)

SPOTLIGHT

Physiology Of Singing

Physiology is a branch of biology that deals with living organisms and their parts. It is interesting to see how the parts of the human body affect our singing. Familiarize yourself with "Physiology of the Voice" on page 65 before studying this page.

Vocal Pitch, Range and Timbre

- Pitch is related to the length of the vocal folds. The longer and more stretched the folds are, the higher the pitch; the shorter and more relaxed, the lower the pitch.

- Range is related to the length and thickness of the vocal folds. Longer, thinner folds vibrate more easily at higher pitches; shorter, thicker folds vibrate more easily at lower pitches.

- Timbre or "tone color" of the voice is related to the size of the larynx, the relative thickness of the vocal folds, and resonance factors (see below). A large larynx with thicker vocal folds produces a deeper, richer sound; a small larynx with thinner vocal folds produces a lighter, simpler sound.

Resonance

- Resonance is related to the size, shape and texture of the surface of the resonators and how we utilize them.

- Some resonators are fixed in size, shape and texture; for example, the sinus and nasal cavities (except when you have a cold!).

- Others such as the oral, pharyngeal and laryngeal cavities, change depending on how we utilize the articulators in shaping the vowels and defining the consonants.

Projection

- Projection is related to many factors. Some of these factors include (1) the amount of air pressure used at the onset of the tone and throughout the phrase, (2) the utilization of the resonators, (3) the amount of tension in the body, (4) the health of the vocal mechanism, (5) the physical and emotional energy level of the singer, and (6) the acoustics of the room.

Die Schwestern

Composer: Johannes Brahms (1833–1897)
Text: Eduard Mörike (1804–1875)
Voicing: SA

VOCABULARY

Romantic period

art songs

lieder

relative minor scale

parallel minor scale

Focus

- Describe and perform music from the Romantic period.

- Describe the difference between relative minor and parallel minor scales.

- Perform music representing German lieder.

Getting Started

A best friend or a bothersome annoyance—a sister sometimes is a little of both. What would you add to the following list?

Sister Advantages:
1. You can share clothes.

2. You can fix each other's hair.

3. You can be best friends for life.

Sister Disadvantages:
1. You may not always get your clothes back.

2. You might have to share a room.

3. You might like the same boy.

"Die Schwestern" playfully describes both aspects of sisterhood with words by poet Eduard Mörike (1804–1875) and music by composer Johannes Brahms (1833–1897).

MUSIC & HISTORY

To learn more about the Romantic period, see page 128.

◆ History and Culture

During the **Romantic period** *(1820–1900)*—the piano became a popular and affordable instrument for many middle-class Europeans. People were able to enjoy an evening of music with friends in their own home. Composers capitalized on this phenomenon by writing **art songs,** *expressive songs about life, love and human relationships for solo voice and piano.* The words and stories for these songs often came from contemporary poets. Since the songs were written in the vernacular (the native language of the people), both amateur and skilled musicians could appreciate their musical and dramatic themes. These songs were especially fashionable in German-speaking countries and were known as **lieder** *(songs in the German language, generally with a secular text).*

Links to Learning

◆ Theory

A **relative minor scale** is *a minor scale that shares the same key signature as its corresponding major scale.* Both scales share the same half steps between *mi* and *fa*, and *ti* and *do*. *A minor scale that shares the same starting pitch as its corresponding major scale* is called a **parallel minor scale.** Brahms uses both the G major scale and the G harmonic minor scale in "Die Schwestern." Sing both scales on solfège syllables. Be especially careful to tune the third scale degree (*mi* in major, *do* in minor) in the parallel scales.

G Major Scale

G	A	B	C	D	E	F♯	G	F♯	E	D	C	B	A	G
do	re	mi	fa	sol	la	ti	do	ti	la	sol	fa	mi	re	do

G Harmonic Minor Scale

G	A	B♭	C	D	E♭	F♯	G	F♯	E♭	D	C	B♭	A	G
la	ti	do	re	mi	fa	si	la	si	fa	mi	re	do	ti	la

◆ Artistic Expression

Write a character sketch for each of the sisters in "Die Schwestern" from the year 1860. Include such details as names, ages, personalities, interests, family dynamics, home environment, and relationship with each other. How can this information help you musically express each verse?

Evaluation

Demonstrate how well you have learned the skills and concepts featured in the lesson "Die Schwestern" by completing the following:

- Choose one verse of "Die Schwestern" to sing. As a duet with a classmate who sings the part opposite of yours, sing this verse a cappella. Use information from your character sketch to musically interpret the verse. Discuss how well you were able to sing in tune and properly express your character.

- Ask a classmate to sing any note. Sing parallel major and minor scales using that note as the starting pitch. How well did you do?

Die Schwestern

Text by EDUARD MÖRIKE
Edited by JUDITH BLEZZARD

JOHANNES BRAHMS (1833–1897)

SOPRANO

Wir Schwe-stern zwei, wir schö - nen, wir schö - nen, so
Two sis - ters we, how love - ly, how love - ly, and

ALTO

Wir Schwe-stern zwei, wir schö - nen, wir schö - nen, so
Two sis - ters we, how love - ly, how love - ly, and

PIANO

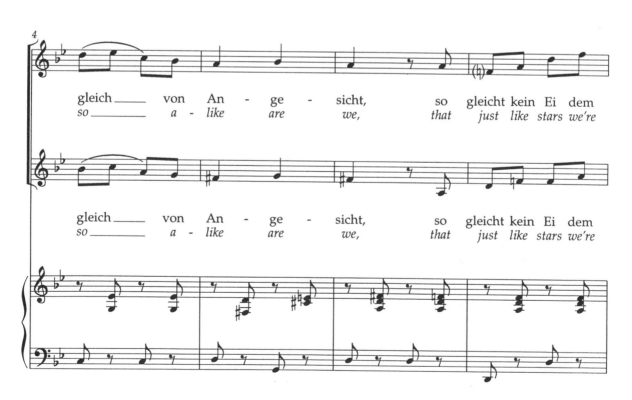

gleich _____ von An - ge - sicht, so gleicht kein Ei dem
so _____ a - like are we, that just like stars we're

gleich _____ von An - ge - sicht, so gleicht kein Ei dem
so _____ a - like are we, that just like stars we're

Wie - sen-plan, dem Wie - sen-plan,_____ und sing-en Hand in
coun - try-side, the coun - try - side,_____ as hand in hand we

Wie - sen-plan, dem Wie - sen-plan,_____ und sing-en Hand in
coun - try-side, the coun - try - side,_____ as hand in hand we

Hand,_ und sing - en Hand in Hand.
sing,___ as hand in hand we sing.

Hand,_ und sing - en Hand in Hand.
sing,___ as hand in hand we sing.

p [leggiero]

[mp]

Wir Schwe-stern zwei, wir
Two sis - ters we, how

[mp]

Wir Schwe-stern zwei, wir
Two sis - ters we, how

f

p

Fire

Composer: Mary Goetze
Text: Patricia Taylor
Voicing: 3-Part Treble

VOCABULARY

Contemporary
  period

imitation

word painting

Focus

- Describe and perform music from the Contemporary period.
- Interpret dynamic markings in the score.
- Understand the relationship between poetry (text) and music.

Getting Started

A Japanese haiku is a form of poetry that uses seventeen syllables of text divided into three lines. Commonly, the first line consists of five syllables, the second seven, and the last five. In describing the subject matter, the poem should also reflect the Japanese philosophy of lightness, simplicity, openness and depth.

Complete this haiku:

> Crackling on the hearth
>
> Hot, alive, it gives its light
>
> Fire, _____ _____ _____ _____.

*To learn more about the
Contemporary period, see
page 132.*

◆ History and Culture

The text to "Fire" is an original poem written by Patricia Taylor, who was only thirteen years old at the time. Later, Mary Goetze set this poem to music. Goetze, a well-known contemporary composer, teacher and conductor, specializes in working with young singers.

"Fire" is representative of music from the **Contemporary period** *(1900–present).* It contains characteristics of the period such as changing tempos, dramatic dynamics and imitation. **Imitation** is *the act of one part copying what another part has already sung.* Also, it is written in a less common 3/8 meter and uses the technique of word painting. **Word painting** is *a musical illustration of the meaning of the words.* Find an example of imitation and an example of word painting in the music. Enjoy learning "Fire," a fast-moving song that captures the very nature of a dancing fire and Patricia Taylor's poem.

Links to Learning

◆ Vocal

"Fire" is written in the key of G minor. Sing the following example to practice the G natural minor scale.

la la la   la la la   la la la   la la la   la la la   la la la   la la la   la

◆ Theory

Clap, chant or tap the rhythm of the following melodic pattern. As one half of the class taps the steady eighth note pulse, the other half should clap the rhythm. Then, chant the text as you tap the steady eighth note pulse. Finally, sing as written.

I   am   fire.   You   know me For my   warmth_ and   light.

◆ Artistic Expression

Sing the following passage several times, varying the dynamic levels as indicated. Maintain excitement and intensity in your singing at all dynamic levels.

Evaluation

Demonstrate how well you have learned the skills and concepts featured in the lesson "Fire" by completing the following:

- Locate the imitative passages in the music and identify the indicated dynamic changes. How can changes in dynamics add expression to your performance?

- Share your haiku with the class. Think of the descriptive words for "fire" used in your poem as you sing. How might this change your performance?

Fire

For 3-Part Treble and Piano

Text by PATRICIA TAYLOR

Music by MARY GOETZE

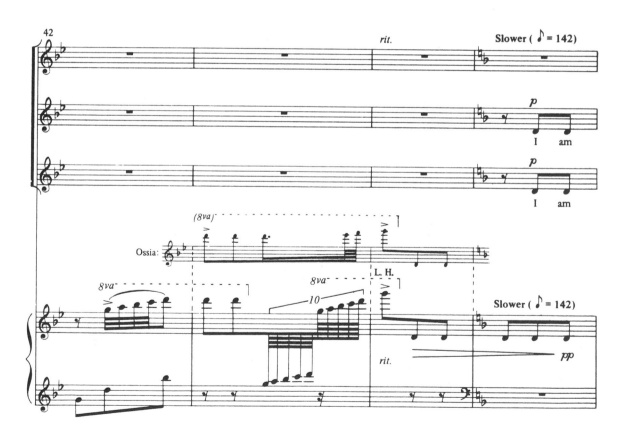

SPOTLIGHT

Concert Etiquette

Whether you are attending a rock concert, an athletic event or a musical concert, there are unique criteria for appropriate behavior at each event. The way in which one shows enthusiasm for a school athletic team or a favorite rock band is very different than the way one would express appreciation for a formal musical presentation.

Understanding appropriate expectations specific to individual events is what allows an audience, as well as the performers, to enjoy a presentation. The ultimate goal should be to show consideration and respect to everyone involved in a performance.

The term that describes how one is expected to behave in a formal music concert is *concert etiquette*. Let's examine behavior criteria specific to a formal concert.

- Wait outside the auditorium until a break in the music or until the audience is clapping to enter the hall if you arrive late.

- Wait to exit the hall until a break in the musical selections if a personal emergency occurs.

- Audience members will hear and enjoy the concert if everyone remains quiet and still throughout the performance.

- Take your cue from the performers or conductor and wait for an invitation when it comes to audience participation.

- Affirm your appreciation of the performance by applauding at the end of a selection of music and when the conductor's hands are lowered.

- Cellular telephones and pagers should be set so that no audible sound can be heard. Better yet, turn them off!

Understanding the uniqueness between various events is the first step toward knowing the behavior expectations particular to individual performances. When these guidelines are followed, everyone's enjoyment will be enhanced.

Music & History

Links to Music

Renaissance Period **116**

    Domine Fili Unigenite **48**

Baroque Period **120**

    Vere Languores Nostros **76**

Classical Period **124**

    Overture to *Die Zauberflöte* **82**

Romantic Period **128**

    Die Schwestern **94**

Contemporary Period **132**

    Fire **104**

Italian painter Leonardo da Vinci (1452–1519) was a genius who showed great skill in everything he tried. In *Ginevra de' Benci*, he uses a blending of light and dark values. The subtle changes in the light make the sad face seem three-dimensional. Notice how the figure of the woman stands out dramatically against the dark background. It is interesting to speculate about who this woman is and why she is so sad.

Leonardo da Vinci. *Ginevra de' Benci.* c. 1474. Oil on panel. 38.1 x 37.0 cm (15 x 14 9/16"). National Gallery of Art, Washington, D. C. Ailsa Mellon Bruce Fund.

Focus

- Describe the Renaissance Period, including important developments.
- Describe characteristics of Renaissance music

The Renaissance— A Time of Discovery

Renaissance means "rebirth" or "renewal." The **Renaissance period** *(1430–1600)* was a time of rapid development in exploration, science, art and music. Vasco de Gama first rounded the coast of Africa from Europe to reach India. Christopher Columbus found the Americas, and Ferdinand Magellan circumnavigated the globe. The compass and first maps for navigation were developed and were used to find and chart new lands.

The greatest invention of the Renaissance (and perhaps the most important invention to modern civilization) was the movable type printing press. For the first time, books, music and maps could be created quickly and inexpensively, making them available to larger segments of the population. As a result, news was easily accessible and ideas were embraced, since more people could read and afford printed materials.

The Protestant Reformation, in which various groups of Christians left the Catholic Church to form their own denominations, brought about a significant change in religion. Bibles and music were translated from the Latin used in the Catholic Church to the languages spoken by the people.

Painters and sculptors created images and figures that were more realistic and lifelike. Among these were Leonardo da Vinci's *Mona Lisa* and Michelangelo's paintings of the ceiling of the Sistine Chapel in Rome. Sculpture developed from a craft to an art form. Michelangelo's *David* was created during this time.

Scientists were aided with refinements in the telescope and microscope. Galileo provided proof that the earth revolved around the sun, and Sir Isaac Newton explained the concept of gravity.

COMPOSERS

Josquin des Prez
(c. 1450–1521)

Giovanni Pierluigi da Palestrina
(c. 1525–1594)

William Byrd
(1543–1623)

Tomás Luis de Victoria
(c.1548–1611)

Giovanni Gabrieli
(1553–1612)

ARTISTS

Sandro Botticelli (1445–1510)

Leonardo da Vinci (1452–1519)

Michelangelo (1475–1564)

Raphael (1483–1520)

El Greco (c.1541–1614)

Michelangelo Merisi da Caravaggio (1571–1610)

AUTHORS

Nicolo Machiavelli (1460–1527)

Martin Luther (1483–1546)

Miguel de Cervantes (1547–1616)

William Shakespeare (1564–1616)

René Descartes (1569–1650)

VOCABULARY

Renaissance period

polyphony

mass

motet

chorale

madrigal

lute

Renaissance Music

During the Renaissance, both sacred and secular music became more complex. The Renaissance period is often referred to as the "golden age of polyphony." **Polyphony**, which literally means, "many-sounding," is *a type of music in which there are two or more different melodic lines being sung or played at the same time.* Each line is independent of each other, and often, each line is of equal importance.

In the Catholic Church, the two prominent forms of music were the **mass**, *a religious service of prayers and ceremonies*, and the **motet**, *a shorter choral work, also set to Latin and used in religious services, but not part of the regular mass.* In the Protestant churches the entire congregation would sing a **chorale**—*a melody that features even rhythms and simple harmonies.* Chorales are sometimes known as hymn tunes, and many hymns still sung in churches today are based on these early chorales.

There were great advances in secular music, as well. For the first time in history, the popularity of secular music rivaled that of sacred music. One of the most common forms of secular music was the **madrigal**, *a musical setting of a poem, generally in three or parts.* Madrigals were generally performed a cappella, and the text was usually based on a romantic or pastoral theme.

During the Renaissance, there was an awakening of interest in instrumental music. Instruments were not only used to accompany voices, but were also featured in solo and ensemble music. The **lute**, *an early form of the guitar*, was as universally used during the Renaissance as the piano is today.

Performance Links

When performing music of the Renaissance period, it is important to apply the following guidelines:

- Sing with clarity and purity of tone.
- Balance the vocal lines with equal importance.
- In polyphonic music, sing the rhythms accurately and with precision.
- When designated by the composer, sing a cappella.

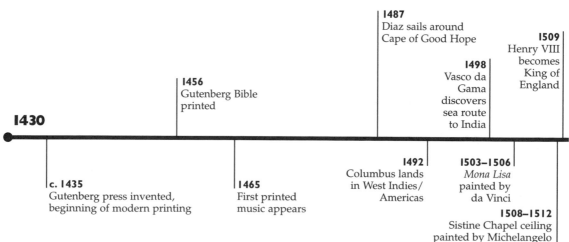

1430

c. 1435
Gutenberg press invented, beginning of modern printing

1456
Gutenberg Bible printed

1465
First printed music appears

1487
Diaz sails around Cape of Good Hope

1492
Columbus lands in West Indies/ Americas

1498
Vasco da Gama discovers sea route to India

1503–1506
Mona Lisa painted by da Vinci

1508–1512
Sistine Chapel ceiling painted by Michelangelo

1509
Henry VIII becomes King of England

Listening Links

CHORAL SELECTION

"O Magnum Mysterium" by Tomás Luis de Victoria (c.1548–1611)

Tomás Luis de Victoria, born in Avila, Spain, was one of the greatest composers of Renaissance polyphony. "O Magnum Mysterium" is a motet that was composed around 1572. The text describes the events surrounding the birth of Christ. The piece features four vocal lines that imitate each other, move together, and weave in and around one another. The texture is quite transparent in the polyphonic sections. Notice how Victoria's use of just a few words during these complex sections make the text easily understood. Of particular interest is the frequent interplay of major and minor chords. Listen to this piece and see if you can hear the contrasting major and minor tonalities.

INSTRUMENTAL SELECTION

"Canzon XV" by Giovanni Gabrieli (c. 1557–1612)

Giovanni Gabrieli spent his most of his life in Venice, Italy, with the exception of the years spent in Munich where he studied with the great composer, Orlando di Lasso (1532–1594). Gabrieli was an organist and resident composer at the Basilica of St. Mark, a huge cathedral right in the center of Venice. "Canzon XV" is written for ten trumpets and trombones. Listen for the contrasts between the contrapuntal writing based on the opening rising theme and the sounds of big block chords. Tap a steady beat to find where a change in meter takes place in the middle of the selection. As you listen to "Canson XV" again, identify and name the different meters that are used.

Check Your Understanding

1. List three major nonmusical changes that took place during the Renaissance period.

2. Describe polyphony as heard in "O Magnum Mysterium."

3. Describe how music from the Renaissance is different from music of today.

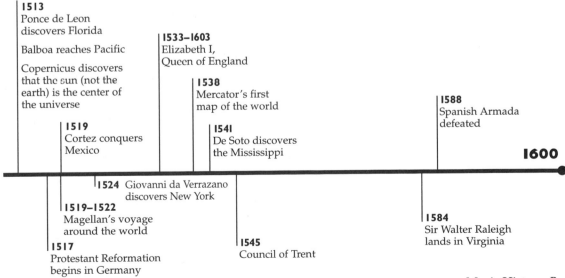

1513
Ponce de Leon
discovers Florida

Balboa reaches Pacific

Copernicus discovers
that the sun (not the
earth) is the center of
the universe

1519
Cortez conquers
Mexico

1519–1522
Magellan's voyage
around the world

1517
Protestant Reformation
begins in Germany

1524 Giovanni da Verrazano
discovers New York

1533–1603
Elizabeth I,
Queen of England

1538
Mercator's first
map of the world

1541
De Soto discovers
the Mississippi

1545
Council of Trent

1588
Spanish Armada
defeated

1584
Sir Walter Raleigh
lands in Virginia

1600

MUSIC&ART

French painter Jean Antoine Watteau (1684–1721) became the court painter to King Louis XV. He is best known for paintings of characters of scenes from the theater as well as for paintings that show the French aristocracy at play. *The Scale of Love* depicts a guitar player in a brightly colored theatrical costume with a girl seated at his feet as the main focal point. A marble bust of a bearded philosopher appears above the musician, turned to the right where secondary figures, engaged in their own pursuits, pay no attention to the two main actors.

Jean-Antoine Watteau. *The Scale of Love.* c. 1715-18. Oil on canvas. 50.8 x 59.7 cm (19 15/16 x 23 1/2"). National Gallery, London, United Kingdom.

Focus

- Describe the Baroque Period, including important developments of the time
- Describe characteristics of Baroque music.

The Baroque Period— A Time of Elaboration

The **Baroque period** *(1600–1750)* began in Italy as a result of the Catholic Counter Reformation. This movement was in reaction to the Protestant Reformation of the Renaissance Period. The Church and its wealthy followers sought to impress the world and re-establish the Catholic Church's influence in political and everyday life. The movement soon spread to all of Europe.

The period is characterized by grandeur and opulence, especially among royalty and the upper classes. Elaborate decoration was used in music, art, architecture and fashion. The term *baroque* has its origin's from the French word for "imperfect or irregular pearls." These pearls were often used as decorations on clothing of the period.

Exploration of the world continued and colonies were established in new worlds, thus creating European empires. As goods were brought to Europe from far away lands, a new wealthy merchant class was created.

Support for the arts was high during this time. The nobility sought to have artists, musicians, playwrights and actors in residence, a form of patronage previously seen only in the church and among royalty. However, the public still had little access to the arts, even though the first concerts for which admission was charged occurred during this time. Music and art remained in the church and in the homes of the powerful and wealthy ruling class.

Important scientific discoveries and theories came from this time. Galileo continued his work in astronomy and physics, and Sir Isaac Newton published *Mathematica Principia*, in which he stated the fundamental laws of gravity and motion. Many consider Newton's book to be among the most important scientific book ever written.

COMPOSERS

Johann Pachelbel
(1653–1706)

Henry Purcell
(1659–1695)

Antonio Vivaldi
(1678–1741)

Johann Sebastian Bach
(1685–1750)

George Frideric Handel
(1685–1759)

ARTISTS

Peter Paul Rubens
(1577–1640)

Anthony van Dyck
(1599–1641)

Rembrandt van Rijn
(1606–1669)

Jan Vermeer
(1632–1675)

Jean-Antoine Watteau
(1684–1721)

AUTHORS

John Milton
(1608–1674)

Molière
(1622–1673)

Daniel Defoe
(1550–1731)

Jonathan Swift
(1667–1745)

Samuel Johnson
(1709–1784)

VOCABULARY

Baroque period

homophony

recitatives

figured bass

concerto grosso

opera

oratorio

program music

Baroque Music

Music of the Baroque period had a dramatic flair and a strong sense of movement. The quiet a cappella style of the Renaissance gave way to large-scale productions and overall grandeur. Independent instrumental styles evolved, leading to the development of formalized orchestras.

Homophony, *a type of music in which there are two or more parts with similar or identical rhythms being sung or played at the same time,* was very popular during the Baroque period as composers revolted against the polyphony of earlier times.

Other important distinguishing developments in music during the Baroque period were:
- The performance of dramatic **recitatives,** or *vocal solos where the natural inflections of speech are imitated.*
- The singing of solo songs which were homophonic vocal compositions with accompaniment.
- The use of **figured bass,** which is *a set of numbers which are written below the bass line of a piece of music.* These numbers represent different chords and indicate harmonic progressions as a guide for accompanists.

An important form of music in the period was the **concerto grosso,** *a multi-movement composition for a group of solo instruments and orchestra.* Other large works that were developed during this time included the **opera,** *a combination of singing, instrumental music, dancing, and drama that tells a story* and the **oratorio,** *a composition for solo voices, chorus and orchestra, that was an extended dramatic work on a literary or religious theme presented without theatrical action.*

Performance Links

When performing music of the Baroque period, it is important to apply the following guidelines:

- Sing with pitch accuracy, especially in chromatic sections.
- Be conscious of who has the dominant theme, and make sure any accompanying parts do not overshadow the theme.
- Keep a steady, unrelenting pulse in most pieces. Precision of dotted rhythms is especially important.
- When dynamic level changes occur, all vocal lines need to change together.

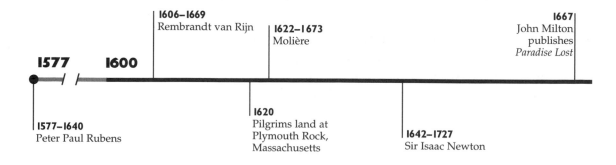

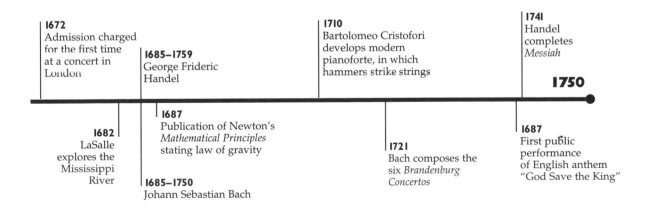

Listening Links

CHORAL SELECTION

Te Deum (excerpt) by Henry Purcell (1659-1695)

English composer Henry Purcell (1659-1695) came from a family of musicians and as a child was a boy chorister at the Chapel Royal. In 1679, he became organist of Westminster Abbey—a position he held for sixteen years. in his later years, Purcell was increasingly prolific, composing some of his greatest church music, including *Te Deum* (1694). In this work, Purcell added an orchestra and a pair of trumpets, never previously used in English church music. The performance was a sensation. Purcell dramatized the words through the music. For example, *heaven* is sung high by the Sopranos, followed by a very low Bass singing the word *earth*. To stress important words, Purcell often used an extended melisma (hear on the words *glorious, goodly, praise*). Find other examples of the interplay between the text and music.

INSTRUMENTAL SELECTION

Spring, First Movement from *The Four Seasons* by Antonio Vivaldi (1878–1741)

Antonio Vivaldi was an Italian composer. He is best known as the master of concertos, having written over 500, half of them for solo violin and orchestra. His most well-known work is *The Four Seasons*. It is a set of four solo concertos for violin, string orchestra, and basso continuo. As **program music**, *instrumental music that is composed about a nonmusical subject*, each portrays one of the seasons of the year, corresponding with sonnets that preface each concerto. What elements of spring has Vivaldi chosen to portray in his music?

Check Your Understanding

1. Identify three important developments that took place during the Baroque period.

2. Compare and contrast *oratorio* and *opera*.

3. Analyze characteristics of choral music during the Baroque period as heard in *Judas Maccabaeus*: "See, the Conquering Hero Comes."

1672
Admission charged for the first time at a concert in London

1685–1759
George Frideric Handel

1710
Bartolomeo Cristofori develops modern pianoforte, in which hammers strike strings

1741
Handel completes *Messiah*

1750

1682
LaSalle explores the Mississippi River

1687
Publication of Newton's *Mathematical Principles* stating law of gravity

1685–1750
Johann Sebastian Bach

1721
Bach composes the six *Brandenburg Concertos*

1687
First public performance of English anthem "God Save the King"

 **MUSIC&ART**

The second wife of Napoléon Bonaparte (1769–1821) is believed to have owned this piano. A six-octave range on the piano was customary during the early 1800s. Notice the imperial eagles that crown the legs and nameplate. Joseph Böhm, the builder of this magnificent piano, lived and worked in Vienna, Austria.

Joseph Böhm. *Grand Piano*. c. 1815–20. Wood, various materials. 223.4 cm (87 15/16"). The Metropolitan Museum of Art, New York, New York.

Focus
- Describe the Classical Period, including important developments of the time.
- Describe characteristics of Classical music.

The Classical Period—
The Age of Enlightenment

The **Classical period** *(1750–1820)* was a time when, as a result of archeological findings, society began looking to the ancient Greeks and Romans for examples of order and ways of looking at life. The calm beauty and simplicity of this ancient art inspired artists, architects and musicians to move away from the overly decorated standards of the Baroque period. The elegant symmetry of Greek architecture in particular was recreated in thousands of buildings in Europe and the New World.

This time was also called "The Age of Enlightenment." Writers, philosophers and scientists of the eighteenth century sought to break from the past and replace the darkness and ignorance of European thought with the "light" of truth. The spirit of democracy was ignited by the writings of thinkers such as Voltaire and Thomas Jefferson. Their writings suggested that through science and democracy, people could choose their own fate.

These new thoughts and ways of thinking became widespread to much of the people of the day. The desire for change became so strong that citizens in a number of countries rebelled against leaders who did not grant them basic civil and economic rights. For example, the American Revolution, in which the colonists rebelled against the British government, was based on many of the principles of the "Enlightenment." The French Revolution resulted in the elimination of the monarchy and the establishment of a new government and a new societal structure in that country. Monarchies throughout Europe that were not overthrown became less powerful; many of these countries adopted a democratic form of government.

COMPOSERS

Christoph Willibald Gluck
(1714–1787)

Carl Philipp Emanuel Bach
(1714–1788)

Johann Christian Bach
(1735–1762)

Franz Joseph Haydn
(1732–1809)

Wolfgang Amadeus Mozart
(1756–1791)

ARTISTS

Pietro Longhi
(1702–1788)

Thomas Gainsborough
(1727–1788)

Francisco Göya
(1746–1828)

Jacques-Louis David
(1748–1825)

AUTHORS

Voltaire
(1694–1778)

Jean Jacques Rousseau
(1712–1778)

Johann Wolfgang von Goethe
(1749–1832)

William Wordsworth
(1770–1850)

Jane Austen
(1775–1817)

VOCABULARY

Classical period

symphony

concerto

sonata

string quartet

Music of the Classical Period

Musicians moved away from the heavily ornate styles of the Baroque period and embraced the clean, uncluttered style of the early Greeks and Romans. Instead of many melodies occurring simultaneously, as in the Baroque period, Classical composers wrote clearer music in which one melody sings out while the other parts provide a simple harmonic accompaniment.

The Classical period has been called the "golden age of music." Many forms of music—the **symphony**, *a large scale work for orchestra*, the **concerto**, *a multi-movement for solo instrument and orchestra*, the **sonata**, *a multi-movement piece for solo instrument*, and the **string quartet**, *a form of chamber music which uses two violins, a viola and cello*—were fully developed during this period. The growing popularity of these forms of music led to the establishment of the string, woodwind, brass and percussion sections of today's orchestras. The piano, with its greater sonority than Baroque keyboard instruments, began to become an important instrument in Classical compositions.

Performance Links

When performing music of the Classical period, it is important to apply the following guidelines:

- Listen for the melody line so the accompaniment parts do not overshadow it.
- Sing chords in tune.
- Make dynamic level changes that move smoothly.
- Keep phrases flowing and connected.

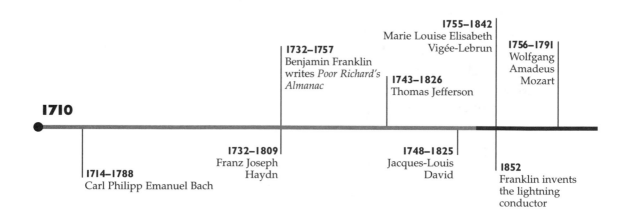

1710

1714–1788
Carl Philipp Emanuel Bach

1732–1757
Benjamin Franklin writes *Poor Richard's Almanac*

1732–1809
Franz Joseph Haydn

1755–1842
Marie Louise Elisabeth Vigée-Lebrun

1743–1826
Thomas Jefferson

1748–1825
Jacques-Louis David

1756–1791
Wolfgang Amadeus Mozart

1852
Franklin invents the lightning conductor

Listening Links

CHORAL SELECTION
"Gloria" from *Coronation Mass* by Wolfgang Amadeus Mozart (1756–1791)

Mozart wrote the *Coronation Mass* for the coronation of Emperor Leopold II of Frankfurt, Germany in 1790. The piece was written for choir, soloists and full orchestra. "Gloria," the second part of the Mass, can be broken into three sections: a beginning, a middle or development, and an ending. Notice that this ending is much like the beginning. The piece ends with a dramatic coda. One melody sings out while the other parts provide a simple accompaniment. As you listen to this piece, pay attention to the innovative interplay between the soloists. List at least three different ways that the soloists sing together.

INSTRUMENTAL SELECTION
Symphony #100 in G Major, Second Movement by Franz Joseph Haydn (1732–1809)

Haydn's *Symphony #100 in G Major* is also known as the "Military Symphony." It is one of two sets of London symphonies written late in Haydn's career in 1794. It calls for a large orchestra for the time, adding instruments from the Turkish military influence—triangle, cymbals, bass drum and bell tree. Listen to this piece of music, paying attention to the contrasting sections.

Check Your Understanding

1. Identify three important developments that took place during the Classical period.

2. What aspects of Mozart's "Gloria" characterize it as being from the Classical period?

3. Describe how music from the Classical period is different from music of the Baroque period.

4. Why do you think this symphony is called the "Military Symphony"?

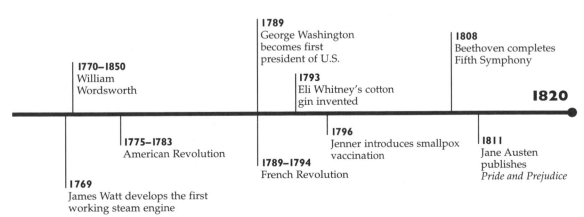

1770–1850
William
Wordsworth

1789
George Washington
becomes first
president of U.S.

1793
Eli Whitney's cotton
gin invented

1808
Beethoven completes
Fifth Symphony

1820

1775–1783
American Revolution

1796
Jenner introduces smallpox
vaccination

1811
Jane Austen
publishes
Pride and Prejudice

1789–1794
French Revolution

1769
James Watt develops the first
working steam engine

American artist Mary Cassatt (1844–1926) is known for her perceptive depictions of women and children. Although born to a prominent Pittsburgh family, Mary Cassatt spent most of her adult life in Paris, France. There her work attracted the attention of French painter Edgar Degas (1834–1917), who invited her to exhibit with his fellow Impressionist painters. In *The Loge*, two women are at the theater. You can see the rings of theater seats and a massive chandelier behind them, which suggests that they are sitting in luxurious boxes.

Mary Cassatt. *The Loge*. 1882. Oil on canvas. 79.8 x 63.8 cm (31 3/8 x 25 1/8″). National Gallery of Art, Washington, D. C. Chester Dale Collection.

Focus

- Describe the Romantic Period, including important developments of the time.
- Describe characteristics of Romantic music.

The Romantic Period— A Time of Drama

The **Romantic Period** *(1820–1900)* was in many ways a reaction against the Classical period, which is often known as the "age of reason." In contrast, the Romantic period could be considered an "age of emotion." A new sense of political and artistic freedom emerged as musicians and artists were no longer employed by the church. The period was characterized by the ideals of liberty and individualism, and of dramatic thought and action.

The Romantic period coincided with the Industrial Revolution. Momentous progress in science and mechanics gave the world the steamboat and rail transportation, and the electric light, telephone and telegraph. Cities grew as nonagricultural jobs developed, and members of the middle classes exerted increasing influence. A new sense of patriotism emerged in Europe as well as in the United States.

The Industrial Revolution produced a wealthy middle class. Their new wealth provided music for the masses to a far greater degree than had existed before. Most musicians' incomes were now provided by the sale of concert tickets and published music rather than by the patronage of the church or royalty. This gave musicians larger audiences and more freedom of expression in their compositions.

The painters of the Romantic period took much of their inspiration from nature. The romantic paintings of William Turner and John Constable express the feelings evoked by nature. Later, Impressionist painters, including Edouard Manet, Claude Monet and Pierre-Auguste Renoir, developed new techniques to bring the sense and feeling of nature alive for the viewer.

COMPOSERS

Ludwig van Beethoven
(1770–1827)

Franz Schubert
(1797–1828)

Frédéric Chopin
(1810–1849)

Robert Schumann
(1810–1856)

Richard Wagner
(1813–1883)

Stephen Foster
(1826–1864)

Johannes Brahms
(1833–1897)

ARTISTS

James Whistler
(1834–1903)

Paul Cezanne
(1839–1906)

Claude Monet
(1840–1926)

Pierre-Auguste Renoir
(1841–1919)

Mary Cassatt
(1845–1926)

Vincent van Gogh
(1853–1890)

AUTHORS

George Sand (1804–1876)

Henry Wadsworth Longfellow
(1807–1882)

Harriet Beecher Stowe (1811–1896)

Charles Dickens (1812–1870)

Leo Tolstoy (1828–1910)

Mark Twain (1835–1910)

VOCABULARY

Romantic period

nationalism

art song

requiem

motive

Romantic Music

Music of the Romantic period focused on both the heights and depths of human emotion. Complexity, exploration and excitement were characteristics of the new compositions. This was in great contrast to the music of the Classical period, which was based on balance, clarity and simplicity.

Many Romantic compositions reflect the period's spirit of **nationalism,** or *pride in a country's history.* Composers used traditional legends, as well as dramas, novels and poems as the basis for both vocal and instrumental works. There was an increased interest in the traditional folk tunes and folk dances of specific nations or regions. For example, German folk songs can be heard in Robert Schumann's (1810–1856) piano pieces and symphonies. In the United States, the songs composed by Stephen Foster (1826–1864) reflected the culture of the South at that time.

Instrumental music became more elaborate and expressive. The symphonies of Beethoven remain among the most popular and critically acclaimed compositions of Western music. Symphony orchestras increased in size, and percussion instruments held a new place of importance.

As the Romantic period progressed, the most important vocal form became the **art song**, *an expressive song about life, love and human relationships for solo voice and piano.* German art songs are known as lieder, and the most famous composer of lieder was Franz Schubert (1797–1828).

Performance Links

When performing music of the Romantic period, it is important to apply the following guidelines:

- Understand the relation of the text to the melody and harmony.
- Concentrate on phrasing and maintaining a clear, beautiful melodic line.
- Perform accurately the wide range of dynamics and tempos.
- Sing confidently in foreign languages to reflect nationalism in music.

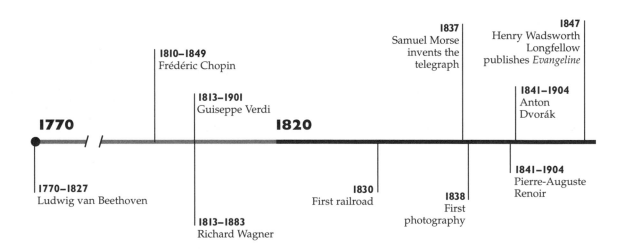

Listening Links
CHORAL SELECTION
"How Lovely Is Thy Dwelling Place" from *A German Requiem*
by Johannes Brahms (1833–1897)

Johannes Brahms was one of the finest composers of the nineteenth century. A **requiem** *(a mass for the dead)* is a piece containing seven movements combining mixed chorus, solo voices and full orchestra. Brahms intended to portray death as a time of peace and rest. "How Lovely Is Thy Dwelling Place" is a setting of Psalm 84, and is considered to be one of the most beautiful requiem choruses ever written. Toward the end of the piece, the opening melody returns. An unusual use of unison octaves is then heard. Describe the various ways that Brahms expresses the words of the text through his music.

INSTRUMENTAL SELECTION
Symphony #5 in C Minor, First Movement by Ludwig van Beethoven (1770–1827)

Ludwig van Beethoven was one of the greatest composers of all time, particularly noteworthy because he wrote some of his greatest compositions after he had become deaf. His *Symphony #5* has been said to be the musical interpretation of his resolution, "I will grapple with Fate; it shall not overcome me." The first movement has an opening **motive**, *a short rhythmic or melodic idea,* that is immediately recognizable. The development of the motive throughout the piece is a tribute to Beethoven's musical genius. Listen to this piece and identify the motive (short, short, short, long). Describe the differences between the first and second themes in this Movement.

Check Your Understanding

1. Identify three important developments that took place during the Romantic period.

2. Identify characteristics of Romantic music as heard in "How Lovely Is Thy Dwelling Place."

3. Describe how music from the Romantic period is different from music of the Classical period.

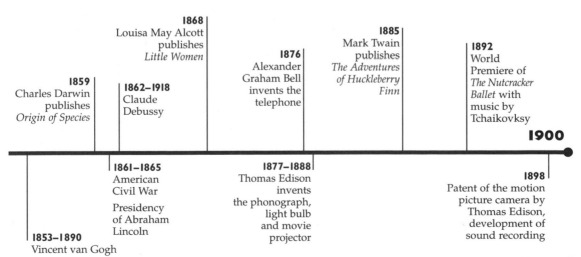

1859
Charles Darwin publishes *Origin of Species*

1862–1918
Claude Debussy

1868
Louisa May Alcott publishes *Little Women*

1876
Alexander Graham Bell invents the telephone

1885
Mark Twain publishes *The Adventures of Huckleberry Finn*

1892
World Premiere of *The Nutcracker Ballet* with music by Tchaikovksy

1900

1853–1890
Vincent van Gogh

1861–1865
American Civil War

Presidency of Abraham Lincoln

1877–1888
Thomas Edison invents the phonograph, light bulb and movie projector

1898
Patent of the motion picture camera by Thomas Edison, development of sound recording

 **MUSIC & ART**

Marc Chagall (1887–1985) was a Russian-born French painter and designer. Chagall's distinctive use of color and form is derived from the influence of Russian expressionism and French cubism. In *Green Violinist*, Chagall reflects on his Russian homeland by depicting the figure of the violinist dancing in a rustic village.

Marc Chagall. *Green Violinist*. 1923–24. Oil on canvas, 198 x 108.6 cm (78 x 42 3/4"). Solomon Guggenheim Museum, New York, New York. Gift, Solomon R. Guggenheim, 1937.

Focus

- Describe the Contemporary period, including important developments of the time.
- Describe characteristics of Contemporary music.

The Contemporary Period—
The End of Isolation

The **Contemporary period** *(1900–present)* has been a period of rapid change spurred by tremendous technological advances. In less than sixty years, aviation progressed from the first airplane to space exploration and man walking on the moon. Technology brought the emergence of the automobile, television, computer and cellular telephone. The recording of music developed and grew. Recorded sound moved from vinyl LPs and audio cassette tapes to CDs, DVDs and MP3s. Can you imagine a life style without these modern conveniences?

The world has changed from one of many isolated nations to a world where nations come together to attempt to solve worldwide problems such as war, famines, health epidemics and environmental problems such as global warming. People are also less isolated. Rather than staying in one place all their lives as was most common in other periods, many people move from place to place. Some even move to other countries as well. Satellites orbiting the earth allow people to instantly observe what is going on in other parts of the world. One of the most important developments of the Contemporary period is the creation of the World Wide Web that allows individual computers to instantly connect to other computers around the globe. School students in the United States taking classes in French, for example, can communicate directly in real time with students in France during a normal class period.

Some of the Contemporary period leaders in the arts include:

- Composers—Igor Stravinsky (1882–1971), Aaron Copland (1900–1990), Leonard Bernstein (1918–1990), Libby Larson (b. 1950)
- Artists—Romare Bearden (1911–1988), Marc Chagall (1887–1985), Pablo Picasso (1881–1973), Georgia O'Keeffe (1887–1986), Andy Warhol (1930–1987)
- Dancers—Martha Graham (1894–1991) and Bella Zewinsky (b. 1917)

COMPOSERS

Ralph Vaughan Williams (1872–1958)

Béla Bartók (1881–1945)

Igor Stravinsky (1882–1971)

Heitor Villa-Lobos (1887–1959)

William Grant Still (1895–1978)

Francis Poulenc (1899–1963)

Aaron Copland (1900–1990)

ARTISTS

Pablo Picasso (1881–1973)

Diego Rivera (1886–1957)

Marc Chagall (1887–1985)

Georgia O'Keeffe (1887–1986)

Jacob Lawrence (1917–2000)

Andrew Wyeth (b. 1917)

AUTHORS

Robert Frost (1874–1963)

Virginia Woolf (1882–1941)

Ernest Hemingway (1899–1961)

James Baldwin (1924–1997)

Gabriel García Márquez (b. 1928)

VOCABULARY

Contemporary period

dissonance

improvisation

fusion

polyrhythms

Music of the Contemporary Period

By the turn of the twentieth century, musicians of all nationalities were searching for original forms of expression. During the first half of the century, nationalism continued to have a large influence. The study of folk songs in their countries enhanced the music of many composers, like Ralph Vaughan Williams (England), Aaron Copland (United States), Béla Bartók (Hungary), and Hector Villa-Lobos (Brazil).

Three major elements that are often heard in Contemporary music include: (1) harmonies that emphasize **dissonance**, *a combination of tones that sounds harsh and unstable*, (2) melodies with angular contours, and (3) rhythms featuring irregular patterns and shifting meters.

During the mid-twentieth century, there was a shift in classical music. Composer Philip Glass (b. 1937) was searching for a new way of writing. He began to compose music that explored the repetition of simple rhythms and minimal melodies. This new form of writing is call **minimalism**. It is *tonal music that stresses the element of repetition with changes that are dictated by a rule or system.*

Also during this period, many different popular music styles emerged. The list below identifies some of the more important ones.

- Musical Theater—centered on Broadway and Hollywood musicals
- Jazz—strong rhythmic and harmonic structures supporting solo and ensemble improvisation
- Rock—music with strongly accented or emphasized beats
- Reggae—a **fusion** (*a combination of blending of different genres of music*) of rock and Jamaican rhythms, instruments, and language
- Tejano—a fusion of Mexican and country music

Performance Links

When performing music of the Contemporary period, it is important to apply the following guidelines:
- Sing on pitch, even in extreme parts of your range.
- Tune intervals carefully in the skips found in many melodic lines.
- Sing changing meters and unusual rhythm patterns precisely.
- Perform accurately the wide range in dynamics and tempos.
- Perform accurately the wide range in dynamics and tempos.

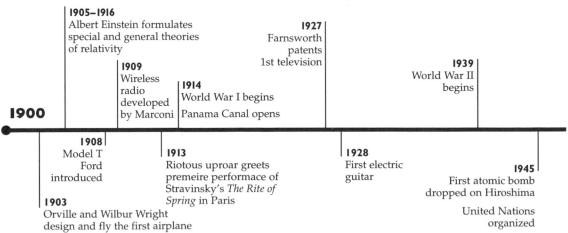

Listening Links

CHORAL SELECTION

"Laudamus te" from *Gloria* by Francis Poulenc (1899–1963)

Francis Poulenc was one of France's most colorful twentieth century composers. His style was greatly influenced by Stravinsky, Vivaldi, Palestrina and Victoria. Poulenc's writing is fundamentally tonal, but his music is full of sudden changes in key signatures, dynamics, rhythms and harmonies. He often worked in short musical phrases, repeating them with subtle variations. *Gloria*, written in 1959, is one of his most popular works. He deliberately contrasts text and musical accents. Combinations of different musical styles, accents in all the wrong places, and beautiful melodies make the *Gloria* a Poulenc masterpiece. Discuss how the repeated phrase "Laudamus te" is treated differently on each repetition.

INSTRUMENTAL SELECTION

"Street in a Frontier Town" from *Billy the Kid* by Copland (1900–1990)

Aaron Copland is one of the most famous composers of the twentieth century. Copland was born in Brooklyn, New York, and was famous for adapting American folk themes into his orchestral works. *Billy the Kid* is one such example. Written as a ballet to tell the story of the outlaw Billy the Kid, Copland divides the saga into six parts: "The Open Prairie," "Street in a Frontier Town," "Prairie Night," "Gun Battle," "Celebration," and "Billy's Death." In "Street in a Frontier Town," many American folk songs are used. Copland adapts these folk songs, and uses interesting **polyrhythms**, or *a technique in which several different rhythms are performed at the same time.* Listen to this selection. What folk songs and melodies do you recognize?

Check Your Understanding

1. Identify three important developments that took place during the Contemporary period.

2. Describe musical characteristics of the Contemporary period as heard in *Gloria*: "Laudamus te" by Francis Poulenc.

3. Describe how music from the Contemporary period is different from music of the Romantic period.

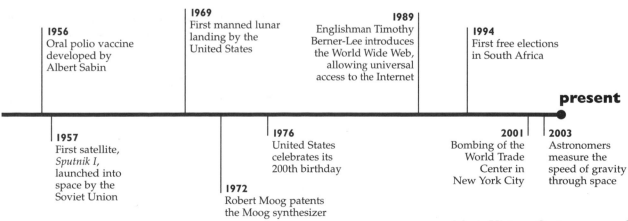

1956
Oral polio vaccine developed by Albert Sabin

1957
First satellite, *Sputnik I*, launched into space by the Soviet Union

1969
First manned lunar landing by the United States

1972
Robert Moog patents the Moog synthesizer

1976
United States celebrates its 200th birthday

1989
Englishman Timothy Berner-Lee introduces the World Wide Web, allowing universal access to the Internet

1994
First free elections in South Africa

present

2001
Bombing of the World Trade Center in New York City

2003
Astronomers measure the speed of gravity through space

Music History *Contemporary* **135**

SPOTLIGHT

Careers In Music

Music Industry

The music industry provides career opportunities that encompass the area of business as well as music. This article will focus on music publishing, retail sales and instrumental sales.

Music publishing involves the process of finding music to publish, preparing the music for print (editing and proofreading), marketing and distributing the music for sales, and supporting the composers for their contribution. The skills required for this type of job may vary greatly. On the business side of the company, training in business, accounting, marketing, advertising and sales would be necessary. The ability to communicate, both in writing and orally, is vital in business. On the editorial side, there are job opportunities as editors, proofreaders, graphic designers and music engravers. Some of these jobs require a music background, as well as writing skills and possible specific computer skills. Quite often there will be on-the-job training to learn the mechanical techniques and specialized software systems used at the company.

Music retail sales requires music experience or training specific to the area of sales. Music stores may feature different instruments, pianos, vocal music, textbooks or accessories. Anyone considering a career in instrumental sales should have a working knowledge of the instruments and be able to demonstrate on the instrument for the customer. The same is true for the other area of sales—one must have a working knowledge of the item being sold. Another position in music retail sales is that of the store manager, who oversees the entire operation of the store. This would require skills in business, management and inventory control. It would also require the hiring and training of new employees. Anyone interested in this field should have a background in business and a working knowledge of music.

An instrument sales representative is someone who represents an instrument manufacturing company. While the position requires skills in sales, it is also important to have an in-depth knowledge of the instrument, skill in playing the instrument, and a passion for the instrument or music in general. The salesperson will most likely be required to work in the field. This involves hard work and possibly time away from home. In addition to music training, a sales representative must also have skills in sales, accounting and bookkeeping.

Choral Library

Ah! si mon moine voulait danser! **138**

El Pambiche Lento **152**

He's Gone Away **170**

Hoj, Hura, Hoj **176**

Music Down In My Soul **186**

O Vos Omnes **198**

Psalm 100 .... **204**

Sebben, crudele **220**

See The Gipsies **232**

Sing A New Song **240**

Sing A Song Of Sixpence **246**

When I Fall In Love **259**

Ah! si mon moine voulait danser!

Composer: French-Canadian Folk Song, arranged by Donald Patriquin (b. 1938)
Text: French-Canadian Folk Song
Voicing: SSAA

VOCABULARY

folk song

strophic form

glissando

$\frac{2}{4}$ meter

SPOTLIGHT

To learn more about arranging, see page 151.

Focus

• Read and perform music in G major and A major.

• Describe musical form (strophic).

• Perform music representing the French-Canadian culture.

Getting Started

A **folk song** is *a song that describes a certain place or event and is passed down by oral tradition.* As a result, there are often different versions of the same song. Traditionally, "Ah! si mon moine voulait danser!" tells the story about a young girl who encourages a reluctant village monk to dance. In the children's version of the song, the words describe a wooden top that is dancing and spinning. Whether singing about a dancing monk or a spinning top, enjoy this choral arrangement of "Ah! si mon moine voulait danser!," a popular French-Canadian folk song from Quebec.

◆ History and Culture

"Ah! si mon moine voulait danser!" is from a set entitled *Six Songs of Early Canada,* arranged by Canadian composer Donald Patriquin. In this set, the songs are arranged both historically and geographically. It begins with a song representing Canada's First Nations and then, starting in Newfoundland, moves across Canada from east to west. Some of the songs are indigenous and deal with local events, while others reflect the traditions of the many cultures that are a part of Canada. "Ah! si mon moine voulait danser!" represents the large French population of Quebec.

This song is written in **strophic form,** *a form in which the melody repeats while the words change from verse to verse.* To provide contrast, the arranger has added the **glissando** (*a rapid scale produced by sliding from one note to another*), legato versus rhythmic singing, and dynamic contrast. Find examples of each in the music.

Links to Learning

◆ **Vocal**

Read and perform the following example to establish the key of G major. This example outlines the basic melody of this folk song.

sol do mi mi re do re re mi   do mi mi re do   re re do sol   sol fa mi mi

sol mi mi   sol sol mi mi   sol   mi re   do mi mi re do   re re mi re   do

◆ **Theory**

Read and perform the following rhythmic pattern in ²⁄₄ **meter,** *a time signature in which there are two beats per measure and the quarter note receives the beat.* Make a distinction between the eighth note pickups and the sixteenth note pickups.

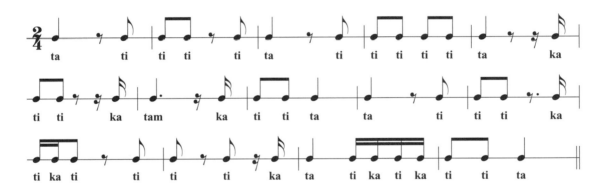

ta   ti ti ti   ti ta   ti   ti ti ti ti   ta   ka

ti ti   ka tam   ka ti ti ta   ta   ti ti ti   ka

ti ka ti   ti   ti   ti   ka   ta   ti ka ti ka ti   ti   ta

◆ **Artistic Expression**

Perform the following example with exaggerated accents. Find this pattern in the music.

Dan - se,   dan - se,   dan - se,   dan - se,   dan - se,   dan - se,   dan - se,   dan - se

Evaluation

Demonstrate how well you have learned the skills and concepts featured in the lesson "Ah! si mon moine voulait danser!" by completing the following:

- Sing measures 114–122 on solfège syllables to show your ability to read music notation in the key of A major. How well did you do?

- Locate the five verses in this strophic song. Describe how each verse is treated differently to provide contrast. Share your findings with a classmate.

Choral Library *Ah! si mon moine voulait danser!* **139**

Ah! si mon moine voulait danser!

For SSAA and Piano

Arranged by DONALD PATRIQUIN

French-Canadian Folk Song

Ah

ais. Bien d'aut - res chos'___ je lui don - ner -

poco dim.

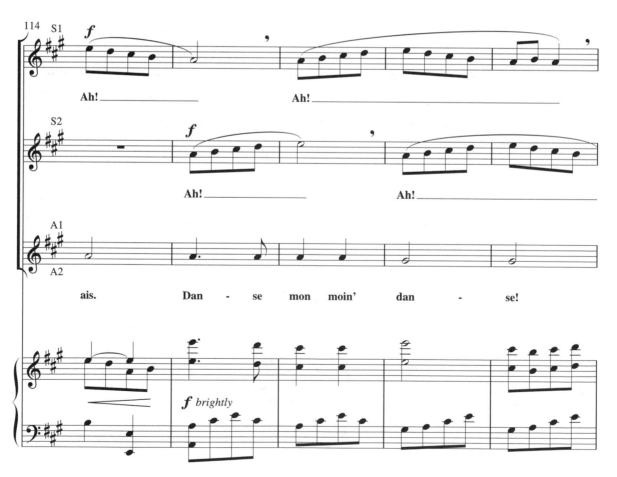

Ah!___ Ah!___

Ah!___ Ah!___

ais. Dan - se mon moin' dan - se!

f brightly

SPOTLIGHT

Arranging

When asked how he approaches choral arranging, composer and arranger Roger Emerson had this to say:

"Generally, an arranger takes the basic melody and accompaniment of a song and prepares it (arranges it) so that it may be performed by a group of instruments or voices. These are things that I take into consideration.

Key

Specifically, as a choral arranger, I begin by finding the best key for the melody. That means finding the scale to use that makes the song the most comfortable to sing. I look for the highest and lowest note of the song, and what ranges would work best for my group of singers.

Melody and Harmony

I then determine the best places for the singers to sing unison or where harmony would be most effective. Using the basic chord symbols as a guide, I like to make the song more interesting by substituting expanded or more colorful chords throughout the song. Depending on the group who will perform the song, I will then write out parts for sopranos, altos, tenor and baritone or bass singers, using the melody and new chords that I have chosen.

Accompaniment

The next step is to create a piano accompaniment that supports and hopefully enhances the vocal parts. Particularly in 'pop' style arrangements, the left hand carries a bass line while the right hand plays chords.

Finishing the Arrangement

The final step is to add lyrics, dynamic and style markings.

There are books that provide guidelines for arranging such as chord voicings and comfortable ranges for each instrument or voice, but most 'arrangers' will tell you (like the commercial says) JUST DO IT! Then listen to the outcome and see if you like the way it sounds. We all began somewhere. Good luck!"

Contemporary composer Roger Emerson has over 500 titles in print and 15 million copies in circulation. He is one of the most widely performed choral composers in America today. After a twelve-year teaching career, he now devotes himself full-time to composing, arranging and consulting.

El Pambiche Lento

Composer: Dominican Republic Folk Merengue, arranged by Juan-Tony Guzmán
Text: Dominican Republic Folk Merengue
Voicing: 2-Part Treble

VOCABULARY
merengue
pambiche
tambora
ostinato
güira

 **SPOTLIGHT**

To learn more about improvisation, see page 203.

Focus

- While singing, add a percussion ostinato accompaniment.
- Sing with correct Spanish diction.
- Perform music representing the Dominican Republic culture.

Getting Started

What do these words have in common?

> *...Santa Domingo*
>
> *...sugar cane*
>
> *...merengue*

They each describe an important aspect of the Dominican Republic. Santa Domingo is the capital city, sugarcane is the major agricultural crop, and the merengue is the most famous traditional dance from this Caribbean country that shares the island of Hispaniola with Haiti.

◆ History and Culture

The Dominican Republic is also known for its dynamic union of three great cultures: African, European and the indigenous culture of the island. *The national dance of the Dominican Republic,* the **merengue**, is a blend of these cultures. It is said to have originated in the mid-1800s. The American soldiers from Palm Beach who occupied the island in the early 1900s were unable to dance the fast pace of the merengue, so the local bands slowed it down. The word "Palm Beach" spoken in the Spanish dialect became **"pambiche,"** or *a dance that is a slower version of the merengue.* An English translation of the Spanish text to "El Pambiche Lento" is as follows:

> "The slow pambiche, how good it is to dance to.
> It is danced in Santiago and in the capital.
> When I dance it, Ay! Sideways what a 'rich' merengue!
> Merengue in pambiche style!
> The slow pambiche I do not dance
> (because) an old lady danced it and fainted.
> Pambiche, pambiche, only pambiche."

Links to Learning

◆ Theory

Clap, play or chant the following tambora drum pattern used to accompany "El Pambiche Lento." The **tambora** is *a two-headed drum played horizontally on the player's lap.* This part is written as an **ostinato,** *a repeated musical figure or rhythmic pattern.*

Clap, tap or chant the following example to practice the **güira** *(a cylindrical metal scraper)* accompaniment.

Walk or step the half note pulse while tapping the tambora and güira rhythms above. Switch tasks by stepping the rhythmic patterns while tapping the half note pulse.

◆ Artistic Expression

With a partner, speak the Spanish text slowly phrase by phrase. Then, speak it again in the rhythm of the music. Increase the tempo at your own pace.

Evaluation

Demonstrate how well you have learned the skills and concepts featured in the lesson "El Pambiche Lento" by completing the following:

- Sing measures 24–32 while tapping or playing the tambora or güira part. Were you able to successfully do both at the same time?

- Record yourself speaking the Spanish text of this piece. Listen to your recording and evaluate how well you were able to speak with correct Spanish diction.

Commissioned by the Glen Ellyn Children's Chorus, Emily Ellsworth, Music Director
for their 1999 Honors Chorus Workshop and Festival

El Pambiche Lento

For 2-Part and Piano with Güira and Tambora

Arranged by
JUAN-TONY GUZMÁN

Folk Merengue
from the Dominican Republic

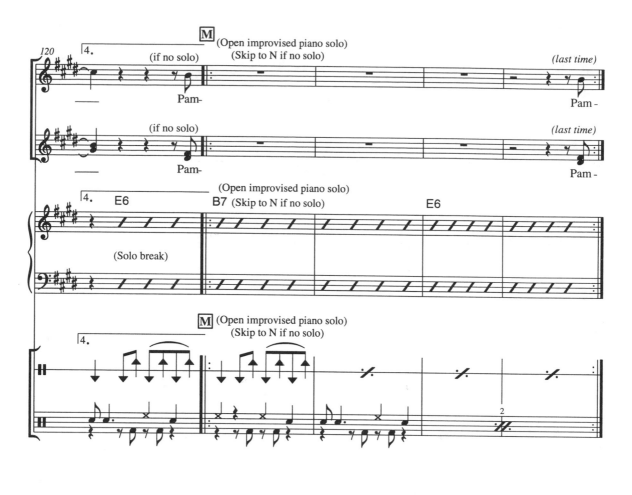

He's Gone Away

Composer: American Folk Song, arranged by Ron Nelson
Text: Traditional
Voicing: SSA

VOCABULARY

folk song

phrase

Focus

- Perform musical phrases with expression.
- Make informed judgments regarding the quality of musical performances.
- Relate music to other subjects.

 SPOTLIGHT

To learn more about physiology of singing, see page 93.

Getting Started

He's gone away for to stay for a little while,

But he's comin' back if he goes ten thousand miles.

Who is "he" in this song? Where is he going? How long will he be gone? Why did he go? What's going to make him come back? This traditional mountain song is a story waiting to be told. "He's Gone Away" beautifully expresses the heartache of separation and the anticipated joy of reunion between two young lovers. Finish this story by giving each character a name, an age and a circumstance. How will your story change the way you perform this song?

◆ History and Culture

A **folk song** is *a song that describes a certain place or event and is passed down by oral tradition.* As a result, there are often different versions of the same song. In the early 1900s, many American scholars began to systematically collect and record our folk song literature. Two famous folk song collectors were John and Alan Lomax, a father-and-son team. In 1911, John Lomax published a collection of songs from the Appalachian Mountains. He discovered that much of the music from Appalachia had been handed down from the Scottish and Irish ancestors. Although "He's Gone Away" is an Appalachian folk song, it is the opinion of some that it originated in England. Enjoy learning this song that represents our American heritage.

Links to Learning

◆ Vocal

To add resonance to your vocal sound, sing measures 3–6 first on the consonant "m" and then again on the vowel "oo." Keep a large space inside your mouth and a rounded shape to your lips as you sing.

To expand your vocal range, perform the following example. Sing the example a half step higher on each repetition.

me__ me__ ma__ mo__ moo__   me__ *etc.*

◆ Artistic Expression

Perform the following melodic example this way: Start with your hands and arms in front of your mouth. As you sing, move your hands and arms forward, away from your body as the phrase expands. Gradually bring your hands and arms back to their original position as the phrase ends. A **phrase** is *a musical idea with a beginning and an end.*

He's   gone   a - way   for to stay   a lit - tle   while

He's   gone   a - way__   for to stay   a lit - tle   while

Evaluation

Demonstrate how well you have learned the skills and concepts featured in the lesson "He's Gone Away" by completing the following:

- Sing your part in measures 13–16 on a neutral vowel to demonstrate a musically shaped phrase. How can you improve your musical phrasing?

- Select one person to serve as the "listener." As the choir performs "He's Gone Away," have the listener evaluate how well the choir was able to sing with accurate pitches and rhythms. Where could the choir do better?

- Share your story from the Getting Started section with the class. Select one story to be read at a performance of "He's Gone Away." In what ways can these stories add to your performance?

For the Pembroke College Glee Club

He's Gone Away

For SSA and Piano

Arranged by RON NELSON

American Folk Song

*Simulate harp by breaking chords

Hoj, Hura, Hoj

Composer: Otmar Mácha (b. 1922)
Text: Otmar Mácha
Voicing: SSAA

 SPOTLIGHT

To learn more about physiology of the voice, see page 65.

VOCABULARY

chest voice

head voice

timbre

duple

triplet

Focus

- Develop a smooth transition from the lower to the upper vocal register.

- Read and perform duple and triplet patterns in music.

- Write and perform rhythmic patterns in mixed meter.

Getting Started

Have you ever walked past an empty gymnasium at your school? Have you ever stopped and called out the word "hello" to listen to the echo of your voice as it reverberated around the surfaces of the room? Now picture yourself on the ledge of a beautiful mountain range. The echo effect of voices ringing from the distance is one of the primary musical effects in this song. As you sing "Hoj, Hura, Hoj," translated "O, Mountain, O," imagine projecting your voice across the vast space of a mountain range.

◆ History and Culture

The Moravian folk poetry dialect in "Hoj, Hura, Hoj" is from the Beskyde Mountains and Valassko region, which form a natural border between Moravia and Slovakia. Here, cattle and sheep herding are common occupations for young men and women. In this text, the men are calling out over the mountains. They are singing about the end of the day, when they will go dancing with their friends.

Composer Otmar Mácha (b. 1922) was born in Ostrava, Czechoslovakia, near the area in which this folk poetry originated. He is one of the Czech Republic's most highly respected composers today. He resides in Prague and continues to write works in many genres. He has, in recent years, written and arranged quite a few significant choral works for the Prague Philharmonic Children's Choir. "Hoj, Hura, Hoj" has become a favorite across Europe and the United States.

Links to Learning

◆ Vocal

Sing the following example to establish a comfortable vocal transition between the lower and upper registers of your voice. Start in a light and forward **chest voice** *(the lower part of the singer's vocal range)* in order to gently lead the tone into a similar sounding **head voice** *(the higher part of a singer's vocal register)*. Avoid a dramatic change in **timbre**, or *vocal color*, from the lower to the upper register.

◆ Theory

Using both hands, tap the following example to establish the difference between **duples** *(notes in equal groups of two)* and **triplets** *(a group of notes of equal duration that are sung in the time normally given to two notes of equal duration)*.

"Hoj, Hura, Hoj" uses mixed meter. Locate in the music each meter change.

Evaluation

Demonstrate how well you have learned the skills and concepts featured in the lesson "Hoj, Hura, Hoj" by completing the following:

• Using the vocal exercise from the Vocal section above, demonstrate a smooth transition from your chest voice to your head voice. How well did you do?

• Sing measures 61–66 to demonstrate your ability to read and perform duples and triplets accurately. Rate your performance on a scale of 1 to 5, with 5 being the best.

• Compose an eight-measure rhythmic pattern that uses at least three different meters. Use "Hoj, Hura, Hoj" as a guide. Perform your pattern for someone else. Check each other's work for accuracy.

Hoj, Hura, Hoj

For SSAA, a cappella

Words and Music by
OTMAR MÁCHA

SPOTLIGHT

Vocal Health

Since our voices are a result of physical processes in our bodies, we need to learn a few things we can do to ensure that our voices will be healthy and function well for years to come.

To experience, explore and establish good habits for vocal health, try the following:

- Limit shouting and trying to talk over loud noise.
- Do not smoke. Avoid smoky environments.
- Avoid beverages with caffeine and fried foods (acid reflux).
- Limit talking on the telephone. Use a supported voice when you do.
- Avoid whispering if you lose your voice.
- Rest your voice if it is tired or if it takes more muscular effort to sing.
- Keep your voice hydrated. Drink lots of water every day and use nonmentholated, sugar-free lozenges if your throat is dry.
- Gargle with warm salt water if your throat is sore.
- Use a humidifier in your bedroom when the air conditioning or furnace is on.
- Try not to clear your throat. Swallow or clear with a puff of air instead.
- Avoid coughing, if at all possible.
- Cover your nose and mouth with a scarf in cold weather.
- Get plenty of sleep, especially the night before a performance.

As you can see, maintaining good vocal health is a matter of common sense in taking care of your body. By taking good care of yourself, you can continue to enjoy a strong, healthy singing voice. Take care and sing long!

Music Down In My Soul

Composer: African American Spiritual, arranged by Moses Hogan (1957–2003)
Text: Traditional
Voicing: SSA

Focus

- Sing in a gospel style using a focused and unforced tone.
- Describe the concept of call and response.
- Perform music representing the gospel style.

SPOTLIGHT

To learn more about careers in music, see page 136.

Getting Started

Think about your music collection at home. Which songs do you listen to when you are really happy? When you are doing your homework? When you are lonely? Music parallels our daily lives in so many ways. Prior to Thomas Edison's invention of the phonograph, people had to make their own music. Such was the case for the early African American slaves who sang spirituals while working in the fields, engaging in social activities, or participating in worship. As a result, there are spirituals that reflect the entire spectrum of human emotions and feelings.

◆ History and Culture

Moses Hogan was born in New Orleans, Louisiana, in 1957, and died of cancer at the age of forty-six in 2003. Primarily a pianist, he became well known throughout the world for his choral arrangements of African American spirituals. Mr. Hogan brought a new and fresh perspective to this historic genre of music by featuring syncopated rhythms, blues-style harmonies, and call-and-response patterns. **Call and response** is *a derivative of the field hollers used by slaves as they worked. A leader of a group sings a phrase (call) followed by a response of the same phrase by another group.* This arrangement is written in the style of **gospel music,** which is described as *religious music that originated in the African American churches of the South and which can be characterized by improvisation, syncopation and repetition.* Find examples of gospel music characteristics in "Music Down In My Soul."

Links to Learning

◆ Vocal

To become more familiar with the harmonies that you will encounter in the piece, sing the following chord patterns.

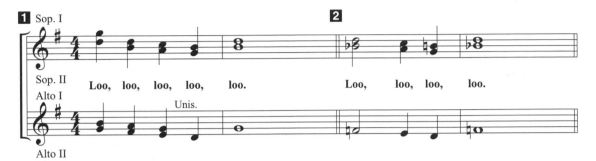

◆ Theory

Clap the following rhythm pattern while marching the half-note pulse. Then, add the text.

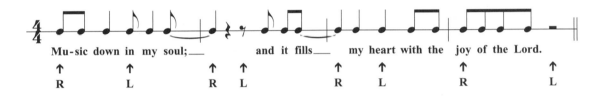

◆ Artistic Expression

Sing the opening measures of the piece with the text, carefully observing all dynamic and performance markings. Can you sing it in an expressive way that convinces others that you have "music down in your soul"?

Evaluation

Demonstrate how well you have learned the skills and concepts featured in the lesson "Music Down In My Soul" by completing the following:

- Record and listen to your choir's performance of "Music Down In My Soul." Determine whether the quality of the singing tone is (1) pleasant and controlled, or (2) harsh and pushed.

- Define *call and response*. Locate in the score examples of call and response.

- Identify the elements of this arrangement that are associated with the gospel style. Name other gospel songs that you know. What characteristics do they have in common with this song?

Commissioned by the 6th World Choral Symposium on Choral Music
for
The Michigan State University Children's Choir
Mary Alice Stollak, Founding Director

Music Down In My Soul

A Gospel Praise Song Inspired by the Spiritual *OVER MY HEAD*
For SSA and Piano

Arranged by
MOSES HOGAN

African American Spiritual

O Vos Omnes

Composer: Thomas Juneau
Text: Liturgical Latin
Voicing: SSAA

VOCABULARY

a cappella

motet

monophony

homophony

polyphony

 SKILL BUILDERS

To learn more about C minor, see Proficient Sight-Singing, *page 122.*

Focus

- Perform intervals with accuracy.

- Distinguish between polyphonic, homophonic and monophonic textures.

- Accurately learn and perform Latin diction.

Getting Started

Have you ever had a favorite pair of shoes that you liked so much you bought them in many different colors? Composers throughout the ages have done the same thing with words. Texts from the Latin mass have been set to music hundreds of times throughout history. Likewise, composers have used other sacred Latin texts, such as "O Vos Omnes."

◆ History and Culture

Historically, European vocal music has its roots in sacred Latin texts. Many of these texts come from poems, scriptures or prayers that were primarily used in religious services. The text to "O Vos Omnes" refers to the prophet Jeremiah's lamentation over the destruction of Jerusalem in 586 B.C. by King Nebuchadnezzar, and the oppression of the Jewish people that followed. The English translation reads: *"O all you who pass along this way, behold and see if there is any sorrow like unto my sorrow."*

Contemporary composer Thomas Juneau has written this version **a cappella,** or *a style of singing without instrumental accompaniment.* It is reminiscent of a medieval **motet** *(a shorter choral work set to Latin text and often used in religious services).* This setting of "O Vos Omnes" changes moods, meters and tempos to fit the character of the text. Juneau also employs many different melodic and rhythmic textures such as **monophony** *(one or all parts singing the same melody and rhythms),* **homophony** *(two or more parts with similar or identical rhythms being sung at the same time),* and **polyphony** *(two or more different melodic lines being sung at the same time).*

Links to Learning

◆ Vocal

Perform the following examples to practice singing the intervals and chord progressions found in "O Vos Omnes."

la   do   ti   la   do   mi   fa   mi   la   ti   la   mi   fi   si   la

Loo, loo, loo, loo, loo, loo, loo, loo, loo.   Loo,   loo,___ loo,___ loo,___ loo.

◆ Theory

Locate in the music examples of monophony, homophony and polyphony. Identify where each device occurs within the song.

Evaluation

Demonstrate how well you have learned the skills and concepts featured in the lesson "O Vos Omnes" by completing the following:

• Divide the choir into quartets with one singer on each part. Sing measures 19–22 to show that you can accurately sing the intervals in tune. Evaluate how well you did.

• Review the terms *monophony*, *homophony*, and *polyphony*. Listen to a recording of your choir singing "O Vos Omnes." On a separate piece of paper, map the textures of this song using shapes and figures that you feel represent the character of each textural device. Share your results and interpretation with the class. What did you learn? How might this information improve your performance?

O Vos Omnes

For SSA, a cappella

Liturgical Latin

Music by THOMAS JUNEAU

*Translation: O all you who pass along this way,
     behold and see if there is any sorrow
     like unto my sorrow. (Lamentations 1:12)

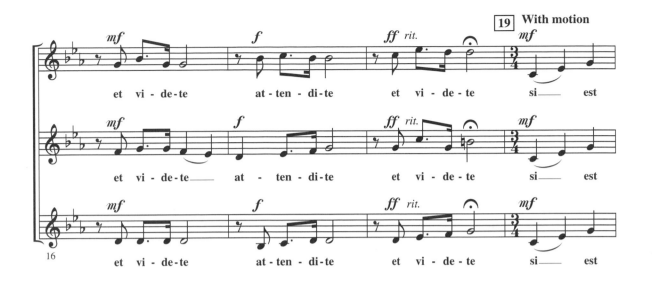

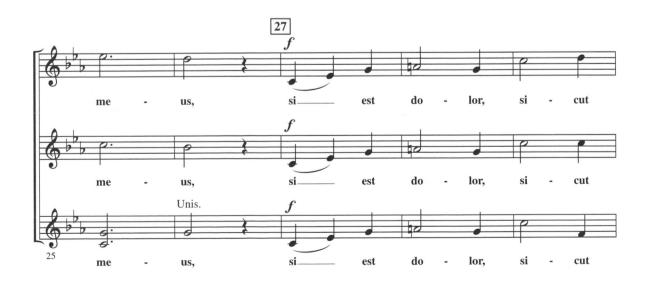

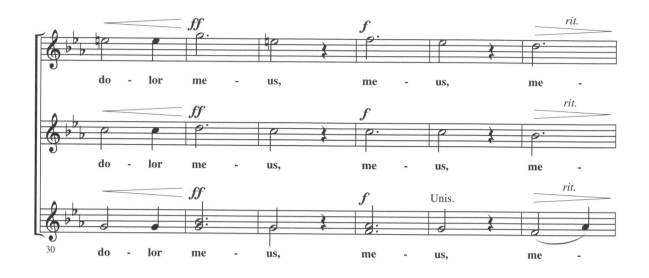

do - lor me - us, me - us, me -

do - lor me - us, me - us, me -

do - lor me - us, me - us, me -

37 **Tempo I**

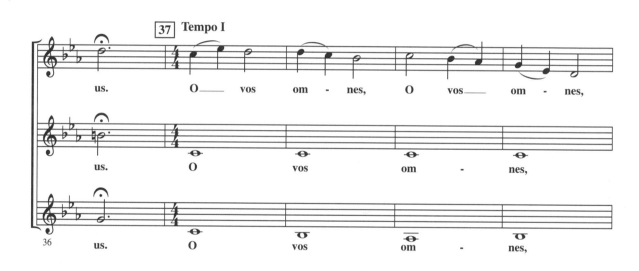

us. O—— vos om - nes, O vos—— om - nes,

us. O vos om - nes,

us. O vos om - nes,

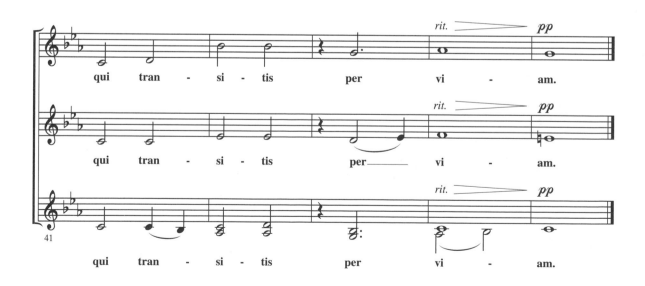

qui tran - si - tis per vi - am.

qui tran - si - tis per—— vi - am.

qui tran - si - tis per vi - am.

SPOTLIGHT

Improvisation

Improvisation is *the art of singing or playing music, making it up as you go.* **Scat singing** is *an improvisational style of singing that uses nonsense syllables instead of words.* Sometimes, these nonsense sounds can imitate the sound of an instrument. Scat singing, especially as a solo, can be the scariest part of singing jazz.

According to Dr. Kirby Shaw, one of the top vocal jazz composers and conductors in the world today, here are some suggestions to help build your confidence in this fun and exciting art form.

- Start your scat solo with a short melodic or rhythmic idea from the tune being performed. There is nothing wrong in having a preconceived idea before starting to sing a scat solo! By gradually developing the idea as you sing, you will have an organized solo that sounds completely improvised.

- Start with scat syllables like "doo" when singing swing tunes. Try "bee," "dee," and "dn" for occasional accented eighth notes on the upbeat of beats (1 *and* 2 *and* 3 *and* 4 *and*). Try "doot" or "dit" for short last notes of a musical phrase.

- Be able to imitate any sound you like from the world around you, such as a soft breeze, a car horn or a musical instrument. There might be a place for that sound in one of your solos.

- Listen to and imitate note-for-note the great jazz singers or instrumentalists. Musicians like Ella Fitzgerald, Jon Hendricks, Louis Armstrong or Charlie Parker can be an inspiration to you.

- Learn to sing the blues. You can listen to artists like B.B. King, Stevie Ray Vaughan, Buddy Guy or Luther Allison. There are many recordings from which to choose.

In short, learn as many different kinds of songs as you can. The best scat singers quote from such diverse sources as nursery rhymes, African chant and even opera. Above all, have fun as you develop your skills!

Composer/arranger Kirby Shaw's music has been sung around the world and has sold millions of copies. As a performer, Dr. Shaw has scatted one-on-one with such notables as Bobby McFerrin, Al Jarreau, Jon Hendricks and Mark Murphy. As a member of the ensemble, he enjoys singing vocal jazz with Just 4 Kicks, a zany four-man a cappella vocal jazz ensemble.

Psalm 100

Composer: René Clausen (b. 1953)
Text: Psalm 100
Voicing: SSA

VOCABULARY

syllabic stress

mixed meter

perfect fourth

perfect fifth

 **SKILL BUILDERS**

To learn more about intervals, see Proficient Sight-Singing, *page 175.*

Focus

- Describe and perform music from the Contemporary period.
- Perform intervals of perfect fourths and perfect fifths accurately.
- Perform text with rhythmic accuracy and correct syllabic stress.

Getting Started

Recite the following phrase, emphasizing and accenting the capitalized syllables:

Make A joyFUL noise TO THE Lord.

Does it sound appropriate? Try this one:

MAKE a JOYful NOISE to the LORD.

How does the sound of this second phrase compare to the first one? Placing the emphasis on the correct syllable is important in speaking and in singing. You will apply the concept of **syllabic stress** *(the stressing of one syllable over another)* as you learn to sing "Psalm 100" by René Clausen.

◆ History and Culture

The text for "Psalm 100" comes from Old Testament scripture. René Clausen (b. 1953) has chosen to set all five verses of the psalm using a tuneful melody and a variety of time signatures. *The technique in which the time signature or meter changes frequently within a piece of music* is called **mixed meter.** These changes in meter often assist the composer in making sure that the stressed syllables of the text fall on strong beats, and that the unstressed syllables fall on the weak beats.

Dr. René Clausen is a composer, arranger, choral conductor and educator. He is the director of the Concordia Choir at Concordia College in Moorhead, Minnesota. In addition to his numerous settings of psalm texts, he has also written other sacred works as well as musical settings of poems that reflect the human condition.

Links to Learning

◆ **Vocal**

"Psalm 100" uses the intervals of a **perfect fourth** (*an interval of two pitches that are four notes apart on a staff*) and a **perfect fifth** (*an interval of two pitches that are five notes apart on a staff*) throughout the music. Perform the following exercise to practice singing intervals with accuracy.

do do mi sol   do ti la sol   do la ti sol   la fa sol mi   fa re do

Sop. I

Sop. II
Alto   La,   la,   la,   la,   la,   la,   la,   la,   la.

◆ **Theory**

Chant and clap the following rhythmic patterns of eighth-note groupings, making sure that you stress the notes that are accented. Once you are able to do this successfully, chant the text as well.

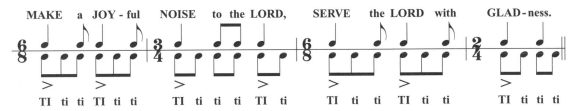

MAKE a JOY-ful   NOISE to the LORD,   SERVE the LORD with   GLAD-ness.

TI ti ti TI ti ti   TI ti ti ti TI ti   TI ti ti TI ti ti   TI ti ti ti

Evaluation

Demonstrate how well you have learned the skills and concepts featured in the lesson "Psalm 100" by completing the following:

- Listen to a recording of your choir singing "Psalm 100." Listen critically for the rhythmic accuracy of the mixed meters and eighth note groupings. Discuss your observations.

- Demonstrate your knowledge of syllabic stress by noting all of the syllables in the piece that you think should receive emphasis. If appropriate, mark them in pencil in your music. Evaluate how well you are able to sing with correct syllabic stress.

For the Kansas Boys Choir, Billie Hegge, Conductor

Psalm 100

For SSA and Two Pianos

Based on Psalm 100

Music by RENÉ CLAUSEN (b. 1953)

come in-to His pres - ence with sing - ing, Al - le - lu - ia,

come in-to His pres - ence with sing - ing, Al - le - lu - ia,

come in-to His pres - ence with sing - ing, Al - le - lu - ia,

Al - le -lu - ia, A - - - - - men.

Al - le -lu - ia, A - - - - - men.

Al - le -lu - ia, A - - - - - men.

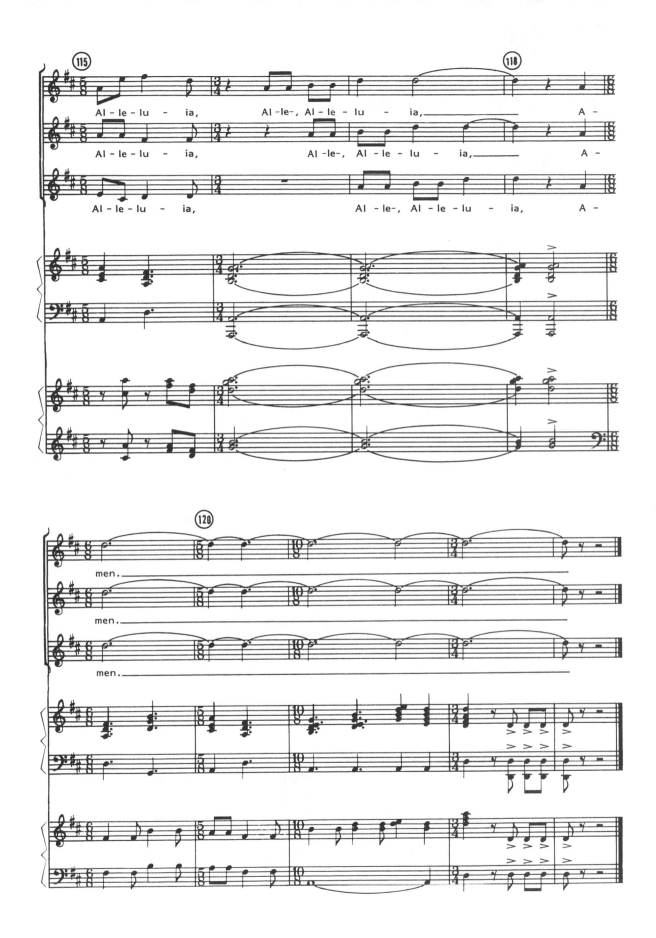

Sebben, crudele

Composer: Antonio Caldara (c. 1670–1736), arranged by Henry Leck
Text: Anonymous, English translation by Henry Leck
Voicing: 2-Part

VOCABULARY

Baroque period
melodic minor
  scale

Focus

- Describe and perform music from the Baroque period.
- Read and perform music in major and minor tonality.
- Relate music to the other arts.

 **SKILL BUILDERS**

To learn more about the keys of G major and E minor, see Proficient Sight-Singing, *pages 71 and 78.*

Getting Started

"Sebben, crudele" has been a popular love song for more than 300 years. Why? For one, the lyrics tell of undying love. A type of love that says, "No matter how much you torment me, I will always love you; and my persistent love will one day win you over to me." Another reason this song has remained popular is that the melody expresses the lyrics so beautifully. Even when performed in its original language of Italian, the sentiment of true love is communicated to all.

◆ History and Culture

Italian composer Antonio Caldara (c. 1670–1736) lived and worked during the **Baroque period** *(1600–1750)*. As a boy, he sang in the choir of St. Mark's church, the most important musical venue in Venice, Italy. Singing in the church choir was the way that many composers during the Baroque period received their professional musical training. During his lifetime of sixty-six years, Caldara wrote an estimated 3,400 compositions. That equates to one composition a week from the day he was born until the day he died! (And obviously, he didn't start composing as a newborn.) Though some of his works are for small instrumental groups, most of Caldara's compositions are for choirs and solo vocalists. In fact, "Sebben, crudele" was originally written for a soloist, but Henry Leck has arranged a two-part version so that choirs might enjoy this wonderful song.

Links to Learning

◆ Theory

Perform the excerpt below to practice singing the G major scale and the E **melodic minor scale,** *a minor scale that uses raised sixth and seventh notes,* fi *(raised from* fa*) and* si *(raised from* sol*).* When comparing a major scale to a minor scale, you will find that the third note is difficult. What other differences can you identify?

◆ Artistic Expression

Love is expressed in fine art as well as in music. Turn to page 120 in this book and study the painting *The Scale of Love* by Jean-Antoine Watteau. Notice the Baroque period dress. Create a story that connects the painting with the song "Sebben, crudele." Share your story with the class.

Evaluation

Demonstrate how well you have learned the skills and concepts featured in the lesson "Sebben, crudele" by completing the following:

- With a group of four singers, perform measures 5–34 to show your ability to sing pitches accurately in both G major and E minor tonalities. As a group, decide how well you did.

- Using the Internet, an art textbook, or your school library, find other fine art paintings that depict the story of love. Share these with the class. What characteristics in these paintings are common to those found in music?

Sebben, crudele

For 2-Part and Piano

Edited and Arranged by HENRY LECK
English text by HENRY LECK

ANTONIO CALDARA (c. 1670–1736)

SPOTLIGHT

Vocal Jazz

Vocal jazz expert Stephen Zegree was asked to share his ideas on vocal jazz. This is what he had to say:

"Vocal jazz is probably the newest and most dynamic trend in choral music education. Traditional classical concert choir literature has been sung for over 500 years, but jazz choir literature has been available to students like you for only the past thirty years. It can be quite challenging to learn, but it almost always is FUN to study and perform.

Why should vocal jazz be an important part of your music education?

- Jazz music was born and raised in the United States. It is our unique musical contribution to the world. It is important to celebrate and embrace the music that comes from our own history and cultural experience.

- The source of much of our vocal jazz repertoire is the songs written by the great American songwriters. Composers such as George Gershwin, Duke Ellington, Richard Rodgers, Irving Berlin, Cole Porter, Jerome Kern and Harold Arlen (and their lyricists) are responsible for the art songs of our country and of the twentieth century.

- Through the study of vocal jazz you have the opportunity to develop your aural skills, creativity and overall musicianship through better understanding of rhythm, harmony and improvisation.

There are many excellent professional vocal groups who have made recordings that I would highly recommend listening to for a better understanding and appreciation for this excellent art form. These groups include The Manhattan Transfer, The Real Group, New York Voices, The Singers Unlimited and Take Six. Some of the greatest solo jazz singers whose recordings and videos you can find include Ella Fitzgerald, Sarah Vaughan, Billie Holiday, Carmen McRae, Mel Torme, Mark Murphy, Bobby McFerrin, Kurt Elling and Nat 'King' Cole.

By all means, make vocal jazz an important part of your musical life."

Stephen Zegree is professor of music at Western Michigan University, where he teaches piano and jazz, performs with the Western Jazz Quartet, and conducts Gold Company, an internationally recognized jazz-show vocal ensemble. The winner of numerous competitions, awards and honors, Dr. Zegree is in demand as a guest conductor, pianist, clinician and adjudicator around the world.

See The Gipsies

Composer: Hungarian Folk Song, arranged by Zoltán Kodály (1882–1967)
Text: Traditional Hungarian
Voicing: SSAA

VOCABULARY

homophony
con moto
andantino

Focus

- Perform music that contains homophonic writing.
- Use standard terminology to describe *con moto* and *adantino*.

 SKILL BUILDERS

To learn more about the key of D major, see Proficient Sight-Singing, *page 104.*

Getting Started

How many folk songs do you know? Can you sing "He's Gone Away," "Charlottetown," or "Shenandoah"? The folk song has been with us for all of recorded history. It is what the name implies—the music of the folk people. It is music that reflects the culture and national symbols of a country. "See The Gipsies" is a Hungarian folk song and represents that culture.

◆ History and Culture

Composer Zoltán Kodály (1882–1967) was born in Kecskemét, Hungary, in 1882. He was very active in collecting and publishing Hungarian folk songs. In 1905, Kodály and his colleague Béla Bartók (1881–1945) set off on the first of many expeditions to collect and gather traditional Hungarian folk music. Together they published several significant books on Hungarian folk music. Kodály is perhaps best known for his work in developing and promoting music education through aural training and solfège musical symbols.

"See The Gipsies" is composed in a homophonic style. **Homophony** is *a type of music in which there are two or more parts with similar or identical rhythms being sung or played at the same time.* You will find two Italian tempo markings in the song: 1) **con moto,** *a tempo marking that means "with motion,"* and 2) **andantino,** *a tempo marking that means "little walking," or a little slower than andante.* Changes in the tempo can add expression and interest to the performance when singing.

Links to Learning

◆ Vocal

Perform the following example with a repeated and rapid expulsion of air in a soft dynamic. Sing using the consonant "p." Then, sing the same exercise on the syllable "zee" in a **legato** style *(a style of singing that is smooth and connected)*. Both styles of singing are used in this song.

◆ Theory

Read and perform the following example that outlines the melody of "See The Gipsies." Locate in the music the voice part that has this melody. Observe how the other voices move with the melody in a homophonic manner.

Evaluation

Demonstrate how well you have learned the skills and concepts featured in the lesson "See The Gipsies" by completing the following:

- In a quartet with one singer on a part, sing measures 1–16 to demonstrate homophonic singing. Listen for precision and accurate pitch. How well did you do?

- Describe how the opening section of "See The Gipsies" that is marked *con moto* would be performed differently than the middle section that is marked *andantino*. Sing both sections at the appropriate tempo. Evaluate how well you were able to show a difference.

See The Gipsies

For SSAA, a cappella

English words by JACQUELINE FROOM
Arranged by ZOLTÁN KODÁLY

Hungarian Folk Song

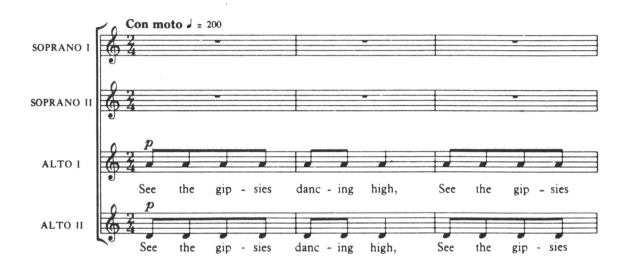

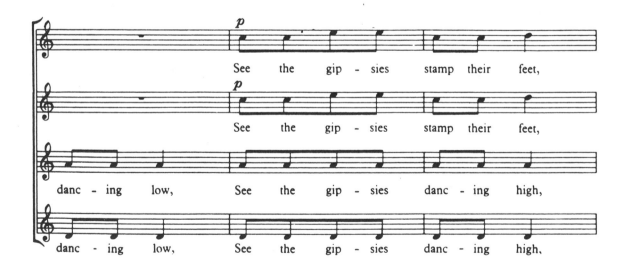

Sing A New Song

Composer: Michael D. Mendoza
Text: Psalm 95:1
Voicing: SSAA

VOCABULARY

Gregorian chant

syllabic stress

triple

duple

triplet

 SKILL BUILDERS

To learn more about mixed meter, see Proficient Sight-Singing, *page 166.*

Focus

- Recognize and perform duple and triple rhythmic patterns.

- Perform text with correct syllabic stress.

- Describe and perform music from the Contemporary period.

Getting Started

Have you ever seen a duck-billed platypus, a kookaburra, or an Australian bearded dragon? You may have seen them at a zoo. What makes the zoo so interesting is the variety of animals found there. Similarly, composers add variety to music by putting beats together in different combinations. Unique note groupings is just one of the interesting features found in "Sing A New Song" by the Contemporary composer Michael Mendoza.

◆ History and Culture

Gregorian chant, or *a single, unaccompanied melodic line sung by male voices featuring a sacred text and used in the church,* was developed during the Medieval period. In 1833, a young French priest named Dom Guéranger undertook the restoration of the Gregorian chant. His work took place on the site of an old monastery at Solesmes, France. He seized upon the restoration of the original fifth- and sixth-century chants with enthusiasm. When teaching the monks to sing these ancient chants, he instructed them to respect the dominance of the text through pronunciation, **syllabic stress** (*the stressing of one syllable over another*), and phrasing. The Solesmes monks also worked on solving rhythmic problems found in the performance of Gregorian chant in the nineteenth century. The ideas about primary note groupings found in the Solesmes method of chanting form the core idea behind "Sing A New Song."

Links to Learning

◆ Vocal

Locate measures 7–10 in the music. Practice chanting or singing this passage with syllabic stress. Place a slight stress on the first syllable of "joyful" and the second syllable of "salvation." Also, emphasize the important words of the phrase.

◆ Theory

Beats are classified into two basic types: **triple,** *a note grouping of notes in equal groups of three,* and **duple,** *a note grouping of notes in equal groups of two.* "Sing A New Song" takes advantage of these basic note groupings in its construction. Perform the following example to practice duple note grouping. Tap the quarter note beat lightly while chanting the syllable "ti."

Perform the following example to practice triple note grouping. Tap the dotted quarter note beat lightly while chanting the syllable "ti." These should be performed as a triple and not a **triplet** *(a group of notes in which three notes of equal duration are sung in the time normally given to two notes of equal duration).*

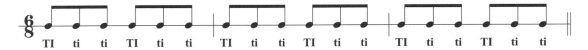

Practice note groupings by lightly tapping the quarter note beat and dotted quarter note beat while alternately chanting the syllable "ti" on even eighth-note groupings of two and three.

Evaluation

Demonstrate how well you have learned the skills and concepts featured in the lesson "Sing A New Song" by completing the following:

- Divide the class into quartets and perform measures 7–14 with the text. While each quartet performs, have the class listen for correct rhythmic and syllabic stress when performing the duple and triple rhythmic patterns. Evaluate how you did.

- Demonstrate an understanding of note groupings by chanting the underlying eighth note rhythms found in measures 7–14 and again in measures 47–54. How well did you do?

Dedicated to Girls '21 (1976)
Cherry Creek High School, Englewood, CO

Sing A New Song

SSAA, a cappella

MICHAEL D. MENDOZA

Sing A Song Of Sixpence

Composer: Michael D. Mendoza
Text: Traditional Nursery Rhyme
Voicing: SA

VOCABULARY

triple

duple

accent

Mixolydian scale

 **SKILL BUILDERS**

To learn more about the Mixolydian scale, see Proficient Sight-Singing, *page 159.*

Focus

- Define and perform a Mixolydian scale.
- Read, write and perform rhythmic patterns in $\frac{6}{8}$ meter.

Getting Started

How many times have you heard someone say, "I've got a song stuck in my head, and I just can't get rid of it"? This often happens with children's songs. Why is it that after a night of babysitting, "Humpty Dumpty," "Jack and Jill," or "Little Miss Muffet" will stay with us long after we have moved on to homework and other chores? Why are the tunes so difficult to erase from our heads? Although the melodies are very engaging, sometimes the real "catch" is the rhythmic pattern of the words.

◆ History and Culture

Contemporary composer Michael Mendoza effectively sets the words of the nursery rhyme "Sing A Song Of Sixpence" to a $\frac{6}{8}$ meter rhythmic pattern. However, the composer alternates the grouping of the eighth notes between **triple** (*a note grouping of notes in equal groups of three*) and **duple** (*a note grouping of notes in equal groups of two*). In the first measure, the beat is felt as two dotted quarter notes (triples), whereas in the second measure, the beat is felt as three quarter notes (duples). The eighth note pulse remains constant, but the groupings are different. You should place an **accent** (*a symbol placed above or below a given note indicating that the note should receive extra emphasis or stress*) on the first syllable of each note grouping.

For fun, can you think of words that fit this pattern? For example, use people's names such as "NAT-a-lie, NAT-a-lie, KA-tie, KA-tie, KA-tie"; or the names of states such as "FLO-ri-da, FLO-ri-da, TEX-as, TEX-as, TEX-as."

Links to Learning

◆ Vocal

A major scale with a lowered seventh degree of the scale has the same sound as the **Mixolydian scale** *(a modal scale that starts and ends on* sol*)*. Perform the following example to practice singing the Mixolydian scale.

◆ Theory

Read and perform the following example using solfège syllables. Begin slowly, and then gradually increase the speed. Find this phrase in the music.

Evaluation

Demonstrate how well you have learned the skills and concepts featured in the lesson "Sing A Song Of Sixpence" by completing the following:

- Using any pitch as a starting note, sing a Mixolydian scale ascending and descending. How did you do? Explain how the Mixolydian scale differs from a major scale.

- Write a four-measure rhythmic pattern in $\frac{6}{8}$ meter. Use triple and duple eighth-note groupings. Add a melody based on the Mixolydian scale. Perform your composition for a classmate. Critique each other's work based on correct rhythms as well as the presence of duple and triple groupings.

For my daughter, Michelle, and the Robert K. Shafter Middle School Choir, Henry J. Wajda Jr., Director

Sing A Song Of Sixpence

For SA and Piano and 2 Clarinets*

Nursery Rhyme

MICHAEL D. MENDOZA

*Clarinet parts found on pages 257 and 258.

When the pie was o - pened the birds be - gan to sing._____

the birds be - gan to sing,_____

Was that not a dain - ty dish to set be - fore the king?_____

Sing, sing,_____ Sing,_____

Sing A Song Of Sixpence

MICHAEL D. MENDOZA

B♭ Clarinet 1

Sing A Song Of Sixpence

MICHAEL D. MENDOZA

B♭ Clarinet 2

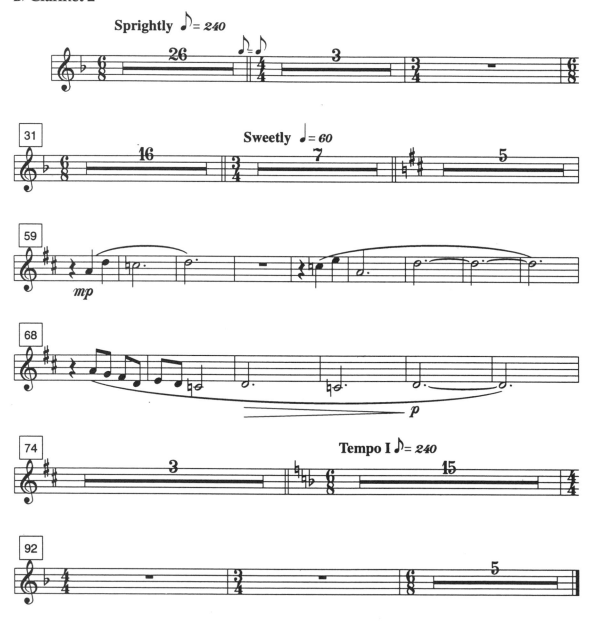

*May also be performed with two oboes. Oboist must either transpose this part down a major second or read from score.

When I Fall In Love

Composer: Victor Young (1900–1956), arranged by Kirby Shaw
Text: Edward Heyman
Voicing: SSAA

VOCABULARY

vocal jazz

straight tone

triples

Focus

- Perform vocal jazz with accurate use of style.
- Perform and create triplet patterns in music.
- Perform and describe music from the Contemporary period.

◢ **SPOTLIGHT**

To learn more about vocal jazz, see page 231.

Getting Started

"Everything old is new again." Have you ever heard your parents or grandparents use that expression? How does it apply to the following songs?

"The Way You Look Tonight" *(My Best Friend's Wedding)*

"I'm a Believer" *(Shrek)*

"When I Fall in Love" *(Sleepless in Seattle)*

Each of the songs above is a classic song that was later re-recorded as a movie theme. "When I Fall In Love" is a jazz classic that was first performed in the 1950s. A more recent version of this song appeared when Celine Dion and Clive Griffin recorded it for the movie *Sleepless in Seattle*.

◆ History and Culture

Vocal jazz is *a popular style of music that originated in the United States. It is characterized by strong harmonies, prominent meter, improvisation, and dotted or syncopated patterns.* The source of much of our vocal jazz repertoire is the songs written by the great American songwriters. Victor Young (1900–1956) was a child prodigy who became a Hollywood icon. He wrote the musical score to over 300 movies! Other American composers such as George Gershwin (1898–1937), Duke Ellington (1899–1974), Richard Rodgers (1902–1979), and Irving Berlin (1888–1989) are responsible for many of the art songs of our country and of the twentieth century. Vocal jazz can be quite challenging to learn, but it is worth it to sing the American classics such as "When I Fall In Love."

Links to Learning

◆ Vocal

Vocal jazz is often sung with primarily a **straight tone** (*a singing technique that uses minimal vocal vibrato*) throughout except for a slightly stylized vibrato at the end of phrases and cadences. Sing the following example on "loo," being careful to use proper vocal jazz technique.

◆ Theory

Chant the following example to practice the rhythms in "When I Fall In Love." A **triplet** is *a group of notes in which three notes of equal duration are sung in time normally given to two notes of equal duration.*

Evaluation

Demonstrate how well you have learned the skills and concepts featured in the lesson "When I Fall In Love" by completing the following:

- As solos, or in a small group, perform the solo line of "When I Fall In Love" at measures 23–30. Listen critically for the stylized vocal quality and characteristics of vocal jazz singing. How well did you do?

- Tap, clap or sing measures 19–22 to show your ability to read triplets in music notation. Rate your performance based on a scale of 1 to 5, with 5 being the best.

When I Fall In Love

For SSAA, a cappella

Arranged by
KIRBY SHAW

Words by EDWARD HEYMAN
Music by VICTOR YOUNG

Glossary

CHORAL MUSIC TERMS

2/2 meter   A time signature in which there are two beats per measure and the half note receives the beat.

2/4 meter   A time signature in which there are two beats per measure and the quarter note receives the beat.

3/2 meter   A time signature in which there are three beats per measure and the half note receives the beat.

3/4 meter   A time signature in which there are three beats per measure and the quarter note receives the beat.

3/8 meter   A time signature in which there is one group of three eighth notes per measure and the dotted quarter note receives the beat. When the tempo is very slow, this meter can be counted as having three beats per measure, with the eighth note receiving the beat.

4/4 meter   A time signature in which there are four beats per measure and the quarter note receives the beat.

5/8 meter   A time signature in which there are five beats per measure and the eighth note receives the beat.

6/4 meter   A time signature in which there are two groups of three quarter notes per measure and the dotted half note receives the beat. When the tempo is very slow, this meter can be counted as having six beats per measure, with the quarter note receiving the beat.

6/8 meter   A time signature in which there are two groups of three eighth notes per measure and the dotted quarter note receives the beat. When the tempo is very slow, this meter can be counted as having six beats per measure, with the eighth note receiving the beat.

9/8 meter   A time signature in which there are three groups of three eighth notes per measure and the dotted quarter note receives the beat. When the tempo is very slow, this meter can be counted as having nine beats per measure, with the eighth note receiving the beat.

12/8 meter   A time signature in which there are four groups of three eighth notes per measure and the dotted quarter note receives the beat.

A

a cappella *(ah-kah-PEH-lah)* [It.] A style of singing without instrumental accompaniment.

a tempo *(ah TEM-poh)* [It.] A tempo marking which indicates to return to the original tempo of a piece or section of music.

ABA Form   A form in which an opening section (A) is followed by a contrasting section (B), which leads to the repetition of the opening section (A).

accelerando *(accel.) (ah-chel-leh-RAHN-doh)* [It.] A tempo marking that indicates to gradually get faster.

accent   A symbol placed above or below a given note to indicate that the note should receive extra emphasis or stress. (>♩)

accidental   Any sharp, flat or natural that is not included in the key signature of a piece of music.

adagio *(ah-DAH-jee-oh)* [It.] Slow tempo, but not as slow as *largo*.

ad libitum *(ad. lib.)* [Lt.] An indication that the performer may vary the tempo or add or delete a vocal or instrumental part.

Aeolian scale *(ay-OH-lee-an)* [Gk.] A modal scale that starts and ends on *la*. It is made up of the same arrangement of whole and half steps as a natural minor scale.

al fine *(ahl FEE-neh)* [It.] To the end.

aleatory music *(AY-lee-uh-toh-ree)* A type of music in which certain aspects are performed randomly. Also known as *chance music*.

alla breve   Indicates cut time; a duple meter in which there are two beats per measure, and the half note receives the beat. *See* cut time.

allargando (*allarg.*) (*ahl-ahr-GAHN-doh*) [It.] To broaden, become slower.

allegro (*ah-LEH-groh*) [It.] Brisk tempo; faster than *moderato*, slower than *vivace*.

allegro non troppo (*ah-LEH-groh nohn TROH-poh*) [It.] A tempo marking that indicates "not too fast." Not as fast as *allegro*.

altered pitch Another name for an accidental.

alto (*AL-toh*) The lowest-sounding female voice.

andante (*ahn-DAHN- teh*) [It.] Moderately slow; a walking tempo.

andante con moto (*ahn-DAHN- teh kohn MOH-toh*) [It.] A slightly faster tempo, "with motion."

andantino (*ahn-dahn-TEE-noh*) [It.] A tempo marking that means "little walking," a little faster than *andante*.

animato Quickly, lively; "animated."

anthem A choral composition in English using a sacred text.

answer In a fugue, the entry of the theme at a different pitch, usually the interval of a fourth or fifth away, than that of the original subject.

antiphon In the Roman Catholic liturgy, a chant with a prose text connected with the psalm, sung by two choirs in alternation. The *antiphon* is usually a refrain for the psalm or canticle verses. Its melodies are often simple, with only one note per syllable.

arpeggio (*ahr-PEH-jee-oh*) [It.] A chord in which the pitches are sounded successively, usually from lowest to highest; in broken style.

arrangement A piece of music in which a composer takes an existing melody and adds extra features or changes the melody in some way.

arranger A composer who takes an original or existing melody and adds extra features or changes the melody in some way.

art songs Musical settings of poetry. Songs about life, love and human relationships that are written by a professional composer and have a serious artistic purpose, as opposed to a popular song or folk song.

articulation The amount of separation or connection between notes.

articulators The lips, teeth, tongue and other parts of the mouth and throat that are used to produce vocal sound.

avant-garde A term used in the arts to denote those who make a radical departure from tradition.

avocational Not related to a job or career.

B

ballad A strophic folk song with a distinctly narrative element. Ballads tell stories.

barbershop A style of *a cappella* singing in which three parts harmonize with the melody. The lead sings the melody while the tenor harmonizes above and the baritone and bass harmonize below.

barcarole A Venetian boat song.

baritone The male voice between tenor and bass.

barline A vertical line placed on the musical staff that groups notes and rests together.

Baroque period (*bah-ROHK*) [Fr.] The historical period in Western civilization from 1600 to 1750.

bass The lowest-sounding male voice.

bass clef A clef that generally indicates notes that sound lower than middle C.

basso continuo (*BAH-soh cun-TIN-you-oh*) [It.] A continually moving bass line, common in music from the Baroque period.

beat The steady pulse of music.

bebop style   Popular in jazz, music that features notes that are light, lively and played quickly. Often the melodic lines are complex and follow unpredictable patterns.

blues scale   An altered major scale that uses flatted or lowered third, fifth and seventh notes: *ma* (lowered from *mi*), *se* (lowered from *sol*) and *te* (lowered from *ti*).

blues style   An original African American art form that developed in the early twentieth century in the Mississippi Delta region of the South. The lyrics often express feelings of frustration, hardship or longing. It often contains elements such as call and response, the blues scale and swing.

breath mark   A symbol in vocal music used to indicate where a singer should take a breath. (**'**)

breath support   A constant airflow necessary to produce sound for singing.

C

cadence   A melodic or harmonic structure that marks the end of a phrase or the completion of a song.

call and response   A derivative of the field hollers used by slaves as they worked. A leader or group sings a phrase (call) followed by a response of the same phrase by another group.

calypso   A style of music that originated in the West Indies and which features syncopated rhythms and comical lyrics.

canon   A musical form in which one part sings a melody, and the other parts sing the same melody, but enter at different times. Canons are sometimes called *rounds*.

cantabile *(con-TAH-bee-leh)*   [It.] In a lyrical, singing style.

cantata *(con-TAH-tah)*   [It.] A large-scale musical piece made up of several movements for singers and instrumentalists. Johann Sebastian Bach was a prominent composer of cantatas.

cantor *(CAN-tor)*   A person who sings and/or teaches music in a temple or synagogue.

canzona   [It.] A rhythmic instrumental composition that is light and fast-moving.

carol   A strophic song of the Middle Ages, sung in English or Latin, beginning with a refrain that is then repeated after each verse. In recent times, the word *carol* refers to a strophic song about Christmas or the Virgin Mary.

chamber music   Music performed by a small instrumental ensemble, generally with one instrument per part. The string quartet is a popular form of chamber music, consisting of two violins, a viola and a cello. Chamber music was popular during the Classical period.

chanson *(shaw[n]-SOH[N])*   [Fr.] Literally "song" in French, a *chanson* is a vocal composition to French words. The rich history of the *chanson* dates back to the late Middle Ages and continues to the present day, incorporating many styles and composers.

chantey   *See* sea chantey.

chanteyman   A soloist who improvised and led the singing of sea chanteys.

chest voice   The lower part of the singer's vocal range.

chorale *(kuh-RAL)*   [Gr.] Congregational song or hymn of the German Protestant Church.

chord   The combination of three or more notes played or sung together at the same time.

chromatic   Moving by half-steps. Also, notes foreign to a scale.

chromatic scale *(kroh-MAT-tick)*   [Gk.] A scale that consists of all half steps and uses all twelve pitches in an octave.

Classical period   The historical period in Western civilization from 1750 to 1820.

clef The symbol at the beginning of a staff that indicates which lines and spaces represent which notes.

close harmony Harmony in which notes of the chord are kept as close together as possible, often within an octave.

coda A special ending to a song. A concluding section of a composition. (𝄌)

Collegium musicum (*col-LAY-gee-oom MOO-zee-koom*) [Lat.] A musical group, usually at a university, that presents period-style performances of Renaissance and Baroque music.

commission A musical work created by the composer for a specific event or purpose. The composer is approached by the commissioning organization (orchestra, chorus, academic institution, church) or individual, and an acceptable fee is agreed upon.

common time Another name for 4/4 meter. Also known as common meter. (𝄴)

composer A person who takes a musical thought and writes it out in musical notation to share it with others.

compound meter Any meter in which the dotted quarter note receives the beat, and the division of the beat is based on three eighth notes. 6/8, 9/8 and 12/8 are examples of compound meter.

con moto (*kohn MOH-toh*) [It.] With motion.

concert etiquette A term used to describe what is appropriate behavior in formal or informal musical performances.

concerto (*cun-CHAIR-toh*) [Fr., It.] A composition for a solo instrument and orchestra.

concerto grosso (*cun-CHAIR-toh GROH-soh*) [Fr., It.] A multi-movement Baroque piece for a group of soloists and an orchestra.

conductor A person who uses hand and arm gestures to interpret the expressive elements of music for singers and instrumentalists.

conductus A thirteenth-century song for two, three or four voices.

consonance Harmonies in chords or music that are pleasing to the ear.

Contemporary period The historical period from 1900 to the present.

countermelody A separate melodic line that supports and/or contrasts the melody of a piece of music.

counterpoint The combination of two or more melodic lines. The parts move independently while harmony is created. Johann Sebastian Bach is considered by many to be one of the greatest composers of contrapuntal music.

contrary motion A technique in which two melodic lines move in opposite directions.

crescendo (*creh-SHEN-doh*) [It.] A dynamic marking that indicates to gradually sing or play louder. ⏴

cumulative song A song form in which more words are added each time a verse is sung.

cut time Another name for *2/2 meter.* (𝄵)

D

da capo (*D.C.*) (*dah KAH-poh*) [It.] Go back to the beginning and repeat; *see* dal segno *and* al fine.

dal segno (*D.S.*) (*dahl SAYN-yah*) [It.] Go back to the sign and repeat.

D. C. al Fine (*FEE-nay*) [It.] A term that indicates to go back to the beginning and repeat. The term *al fine* indicates to sing to the end, or *fine*.

decrescendo (*DAY-creh-shen-doh*) [It.] A dynamic marking that indicates to gradually sing or play softer. ⏵

descant A special part in a piece of music that is usually sung higher than the melody or other parts of the song.

diatonic interval The distance between two notes that are indigenous to a major or minor scale.

diatonic scale (*die-uh-TAH-nick*) A scale that uses no altered pitches or accidentals. Both the major scale and the natural minor scale are examples of a diatonic scale.

diction The pronunciation of words while singing.

diminished chord   A minor chord in which the top note is lowered one half step from *mi* to *me*.

diminuendo *(dim.) (duh-min-yoo-WEN-doh)* [It.] Gradually getting softer; *see* decrescendo.

diphthong   A combination of two vowel sounds.

dissonance   A combination of pitches or tones that clash.

dolce *(DOHL-chay)*   [It.] Sweetly.

dominant chord   A chord built on the fifth note of a scale. In a major scale, this chord uses the notes *sol, ti* and *re*, and it may be called the **V** ("five") chord. In a minor scale, this chord uses the notes *mi, sol* and *ti* (or *mi, si* and *ti*), and it may be called the **v** or **V** ("five") chord.

Dorian scale *(DOOR-ee-an)*   [Gk.] A modal scale that starts and ends on *re*.

dot   A symbol that increases the length of a given note by half its value. It is placed to the right of the note.

dotted half note   A note that represents three beats of sound when the quarter note receives the beat. ♩.

dotted rhythms   A dot after a note lengthens the note by one-half its original value. When notes are paired, the first note is often three times longer than the note that follows (e.g., dotted half note followed by quarter note, dotted quarter note followed by eighth note, dotted eighth note followed by sixteenth note).

double barline   A set of two barlines that indicate the end of a piece or section of music.

D. S. al coda *(dahl SAYN-yoh ahl KOH-dah)* [It.] Repeat from the symbol (𝄋) and skip to the coda when you see the sign. (⊕)

duet   A group of two singers or instrumentalists.

duple   Notes in equal groups of two.

dynamics   Symbols in music that indicate how loud or soft to sing or play.

E

eighth note   A note that represents one-half beat of sound when the quarter note receives the beat. Two eighth notes equal one beat of sound when the quarter note receives the beat.   ♪ ♫

eighth rest   A rest that represents one-half beat of silence when the quarter note receives the beat. Two eighth rests equal one beat of silence when the quarter note receives the beat.   𝄾

expressionism   Music of the early twentieth century usually associated with Germany that was written in a deeply subjective and introspective style.

expressive singing   To sing with feeling.

F

falsetto   [It.] The register in the male voice that extends far above the natural voice. The light upper range.

fanfare   A brief celebratory piece, usually performed by brass instruments and percussion, at the beginning of an event.

fermata *(fur-MAH-tah)*   [It.] A symbol that indicates to hold a note or rest for longer than its given value. (⌢)

fine *(fee-NAY)*   [It.] A term used to indicate the end of a piece of music.

fixed do *(doh)*   A system of syllables in which the note C is always *do*. See movable do.

flat   A symbol that lowers the pitch of a given note by one half step. (♭)

folk music   Music that is passed down from generation to generation through oral tradition. Traditional music that reflects a place, event or a national feeling.

folk song   A song passed down from generation to generation through oral tradition. A song that reflects a place, event or a national feeling.

form   The structure or design of a musical composition.

forte *(FOR-tay)* [It.] A dynamic that indicates to sing or play loud. (*f*)

fortissimo *(for-TEE-see-moh)* [It.] A dynamic that indicates to sing or play very loud. (*ff*)

fugue *(FYOOG)* A musical form in which the same melody is performed by different instruments or voices entering at different times, thus adding layers of sound.

fusion Music that is developed by the act of combining various types and cultural influences of music into a new style.

G

glee A homophonic, unaccompanied English song, usually in three or four vocal parts. The texts of early glees, from the seventeenth century, were usually about eating and drinking, but also about patriotism, hunting and love.

glissando *(glees-SAHN-doh)* An effect produced by sliding from one note to another. The pseudo-Italian word comes from the French word *glisser*, "to slide."

gospel music Religious music that originated in the African American churches of the South. This music can be characterized by improvisation, syncopation and repetition.

gradual In the Roman Catholic liturgy, a chant that follows the reading of the Epistle. The texts are usually from the Psalms. The melodies often contain several notes per syllable. The term *gradual* (from the Latin *gradus*, "a step") is so called because it was sung while the deacon was ascending the steps to sing the Gospel.

grand opera A large-scale opera that is sung throughout, with no spoken dialogue. *See* Singspiel.

grand staff A staff that is created when two staves are joined together.

grandioso [It.] Stately, majestic.

grave *(GRAH-veh)* [It.] Slow, solemn.

grazioso *(grah-tsee-OH-soh)* [It.] Graceful.

Gregorian chant A single, unaccompanied melodic line sung by male voices. Featuring a sacred text and used in the church, this style of music was developed in the medieval period.

guiro *(GWEE-roh)* A Latin American percussion instrument made from an elongated gourd, with notches cut into it, over which a stick is scraped to produce a rasping sound.

H

half note A note that represents two beats of sound when the quarter note receives the beat.

half rest A rest that represents two beats of silence when the quarter note receives the beat.

half step The smallest distance (interval) between two notes on a keyboard; the chromatic scale is composed entirely of half steps.

harmonic intervals Two or more notes that are sung or played simultaneously.

harmonic minor scale A minor scale that uses a raised seventh note, *si* (raised from *sol*).

harmonics Small whistle-like tones, or overtones, that are sometimes produced over a sustained pitch.

harmony A musical sound that is formed when two or more different pitches are played or sung at the same time.

head voice The higher part of the singer's vocal range.

hemiola In early music theory, *hemiola* denotes the ratio 3:2. In the modern metrical system, it refers to the articulation of two bars in triple meter as if they were three bars in duple meter.

High Renaissance The latter part of the Renaissance period, c. 1430–1600.

homophonic *(hah-muh-FAH-nik)* [Gk.] A texture where all parts sing similar rhythm in unison or harmony.

homophony *(haw-MAW-faw-nee)* [Gk.] A type of music in which there are two or more parts with similar or identical rhythms being sung or played at the same time. Also, music in which melodic interest is concentrated in one voice part and may have subordinate accompaniment.

hymn A song or poem that offers praise to God.

I

imitation The act of one part copying what another part has already played or sung.

improvisation The art of singing or playing music, making it up as you go, or composing and performing a melody at the same time.

interlocking Short melodic or rhythmic patterns performed simultaneously that fit together to create a continuous musical texture.

interlude A short piece of music that is used to bridge the acts of a play or the verses of a song or hymn.

International Phonetic Alphabet (IPA) A phonetic alphabet that provides a notational standard for all languages. Developed in Paris, France, in 1886.

interval The distance between two notes.

intonation The accuracy of pitch, in-tune singing.

Ionian scale *(eye-OWN-ee-an)* [Gk.] A modal scale that starts and ends on *do*. It is made up of the same arrangement of whole and half steps as a major scale.

J

jazz An original American style of music that features swing rhythms, syncopation and improvisation.

K

key Determined by a song's or scale's home tone, or keynote.

key signature A symbol or set of symbols that determines the key of a piece of music.

L

Ländler *(LEND-ler)* [Ger.] A slow Austrian dance, performed in 3/4 meter, similar to a waltz.

largo [It.] A tempo marking that indicates a broad, slow, dignified style.

ledger lines Short lines that appear above, between treble and bass clefs, or below the bass clef, used to expand the notation.

legato *(leh-GAH-toh)* [It.] A connected and sustained style of singing and playing.

lento *(LEN-toh)* [It.] Slow; a little faster than *largo*, a little slower than *adagio*.

lied *(leet)* [Ger.] A song in the German language, generally with a secular text.

lieder *(LEE-der)* [Ger.] Plural of *lied*. Songs in the German language, especially art songs of the Romantic period. These songs usually have a secular text.

liturgical text A text that has been written for the purpose of worship in a church setting.

lute An early form of the guitar.

Lydian scale *(LIH-dee-an)* [Gk.] A modal scale that starts and ends on *fa*.

lyricist The writer of the words (lyrics) to a song.

lyrics The words of a song.

M

madrigal A poem that has been set to music in the language of the composer. Featuring several imitative parts, it usually has a secular text and is generally sung *a cappella*.

maestoso (*mah-eh-STOH-soh*) [It.] Perform majestically.

major chord A chord that can be based on the *do, mi,* and *sol* of a major scale.

major scale A scale that has *do* as its home tone, or keynote. It is made up of a specific arrangement of whole steps and half steps in the following order: W + W + H + W + W + W + H.

major second Two notes a whole step apart.

major tonality A song that is based on a major scale with *do* as its keynote, or home tone.

manniboula A rustic pizzicato bass instrument consisting of a wooden resonance box with a rose window on its front panel, where there are three metallic blades that sound when manipulated by the fingers of the player sitting on it. Also called a *manniba.*

marcato (*mar-CAH-toh*) [It.] A stressed and accented style of singing and playing.

mass A religious service of prayers and ceremonies originating in the Roman Catholic Church consisting of spoken and sung sections. It consists of several sections divided into two groups: proper (text changes for every day) and ordinary (text stays the same in every Mass). Between the years 1400 and 1600, the Mass assumed its present form consisting of the Kyrie, Gloria, Credo, Sanctus and Agnus Dei. It may include chants, hymns and Psalms as well. The Mass also developed into large musical works for chorus, soloists and even orchestra.

measure The space between two barlines.

Medieval period The historical period in Western civilization also known as the Middle Ages (400–1430).

medley A collection of songs musically linked together.

melisma (*muh-LIZ-mah*) [Gk.] A group of notes sung to a single syllable or word.

melismatic singing (*muh-liz-MAT-ik*) [Gk.] A style of text setting in which one syllable is sung over many notes.

melodic contour The overall shape of the melody.

melodic minor scale A minor scale that uses raised sixth and seventh notes: *fi* (raised from *fa*) and *si* (raised from *sol*). Often, these notes are raised in ascending patterns, but not in descending patterns.

melody A logical succession of musical tones.

meno mosso (*MEH-noh MOHS-soh*) [It.] A tempo marking that indicates "less motion," or slower.

merengue (*meh-REN-geh*) [Sp.] A Latin American ballroom dance in moderate duple meter with the basic rhythm pattern:

It is the national dance of the Dominican Republic.

messa di voce (*MES-sah dee VOH-cheh*) [It.] A technique of singing a crescendo and decrescendo on a held note. The term literally means "placing of the voice."

meter A way of organizing rhythm.

meter signature *See* time signature.

metronome marking A sign that appears over the top line of the staff at the beginning of a piece or section of music that indicates the tempo. It shows the kind of note that will receive the beat and the number of beats per minute as measured by a metronome.

mezzo forte (*MEH-tsoh FOR tay*) [It.] A dynamic that indicates to sing or play medium loud. (*mf*)

mezzo piano (*MEH-tsoh pee-AH-noh*) [It.] A dynamic that indicates to sing or play medium soft. (*mp*)

mezzo voce (*MEH-tsoh VOH-cheh*) [It.] With half voice; reduced volume and tone.

minor chord A chord that can be based on the *la, do,* and *mi* of a minor scale.

minor scale   A scale that has *la* as its home tone, or keynote. It is made up of a specific arrangement of whole steps and half steps in the following order: W + H +W + W + H + W + W.

minor tonality   A song that is based on a minor scale with *la* as its keynote, or home tone.

minstrel   The term *minstrel* originally referred to a wandering musician from the Middle Ages. In the late nineteenth century, the word was applied to black-face entertainers who presented a variety show consisting of comic songs, sentimental ballads, soft-shoe dancing, clogging, instrumental playing, comedy skits, sight gags and jokes.

missa brevis *(MEES-sah BREH-vees)* [Lat.] Literally, a "brief mass." The term refers to a short setting of the Mass Ordinary.

mixed meter   A technique in which the time signature or meter changes frequently within a piece of music.

Mixolydian scale *(mix-oh-LIH-dee-an)* [Gr.] A modal scale that starts and ends on *sol*.

modal scale   A scale based on a mode. Like major and minor scales, each modal scale is made up of a specific arrangement of whole steps and half steps, with the half steps occurring between *mi* and *fa*, and *ti* and *do*.

mode   An early system of pitch organization that was used before major and minor scales and keys were developed.

modulation   A change in the key or tonal center of a piece of music within the same song.

molto   [It.] Very or much; for example, *molto rit.* means "much slower."

monophony *(mon-AH-foh-nee)* Music with only a single melody line (e.g., Gregorian chant).

motet *(moh-teht)*   Originating as a Medieval and Renaissance polyphonic song, this choral form of composition became an unaccompanied work, often in contrapuntal style. Also, a short, sacred choral piece with a Latin text that is used in religious services but is not a part of the regular Mass.

motive   A shortened expression, sometimes contained within a phrase.

moveable do *(doh)*   A system of syllables in which the first note of each diatonic scale is *do*. *See* fixed do.

music critic   A writer who gives an evaluation of a musical performance.

music notation   Any means of writing down music, including the use of notes, rests and symbols.

musical   A play or film whose action and dialogue are combined with singing and dancing.

musical theater   An art form that combines acting, singing, and dancing to tell a story. It often includes staging, costumes, lighting and scenery.

mysterioso   [It.] Perform in a mysterious or haunting way; to create a haunting mood.

N

narrative song   A song that tells a story.

national anthem   A patriotic song adopted by nations through tradition or decree.

nationalism   Patriotism; pride of country. This feeling influenced many Romantic composers such as Wagner, Tchaikovsky, Dvořák, Chopin and Brahms.

natural   A symbol that cancels a previous sharp or flat, or a sharp or flat in a key signature. (♮)

natural minor scale   A minor scale that uses no altered pitches or accidentals.

neoclassicism   Music of the early twentieth century characterized by the inclusion of contemporary styles or features derived from the music of the seventeenth and eighteenth centuries.

New Romanticism   A genuine tonal melody composed with exotic textures and timbres.

no breath mark   A direction not to take a breath at a specific place in the composition. (N.B.)

non troppo (*nahn TROH-poh*)   [It.] Not too much; for example, *allegro non troppo*, "not too fast."

notation   Written notes, symbols and directions used to represent music within a composition.

nuance   Subtle variations in tempo, phrasing, articulation, dynamics and intonation that are used to enhance a musical performance.

O

octave   An interval of two pitches that are eight notes apart on a staff.

ode   A poem written in honor of a special person or occasion. These poems were generally dedicated to a member of a royal family. In music, an ode usually includes several sections for choir, soloists and orchestra.

opera   A combination of singing, instrumental music, dancing and drama that tells a story.

operetta (*oh-peh-RET-tah*)   [It.] A light opera, often with spoken dialogue and dancing.

optional divisi (*opt.div.*)   Indicating a split in the music into optional harmony, shown by a smaller cued note.

oral tradition   Music that is learned through rote or by ear and is interpreted by its performer(s).

oratorio (*or-uh-TOR-ee-oh*)   [It.] A dramatic work for solo voices, chorus and orchestra presented without theatrical action. Usually, oratorios are based on a literary or religious theme.

ostinato (*ahs-tuh-NAH-toh*)   [It.] A rhythmic or melodic passage that is repeated continuously.

overture   A piece for orchestra that serves as an introduction to an opera or other dramatic work.

P

palate   The roof of the mouth; the hard palate is at the front, the soft palate is at the back.

pambiche (*pahm-BEE-cheh*)   [Sp.] A dance that is a slower version of the merengue.

parallel keys   Major and minor keys having the same keynote, or home tone (tonic).

parallel minor scale   A minor scale that shares the same starting pitch as its corresponding major scale.

parallel motion   A technique in which two or more melodic lines move in the same direction.

parallel sixths   A group of intervals that are a sixth apart and which move at the same time and in the same direction.

parallel thirds   A group of intervals that are a third apart and which move at the same time and in the same direction.

part-singing   Two or more parts singing an independent melodic line at the same time.

pentatonic scale   A five-tone scale using the pitches *do, re, mi, sol* and *la*.

perfect fifth   An interval of two pitches that are five notes apart on a staff.

perfect fourth   An interval of two pitches that are four notes apart on a staff.

phrase   A musical idea with a beginning and an end.

phrasing   A method of punctuating a musical idea, comparable to a line or sentence in poetry.

Phrygian scale (*FRIH-gee-an*)   [Gk.] A modal scale that starts and ends on *mi*.

pianissimo (*pee-ah-NEE-see-moh*)   [It.] A dynamic that indicates to sing or play very soft. (*pp*)

piano (*pee-AH-noh*)   [It.] A dynamic that indicates to sing or play soft. (*p*)

Picardy third   An interval of a major third used in the final, tonic chord of a piece written in a minor key.

pitch Sound, the result of vibration; the highness or lowness of a tone, determined by the number of vibrations per second.

pitch matching In a choral ensemble, the ability to sing the same notes as those around you.

più *(pyoo)* [It.] More; for example, *più forte* means "more loudly."

più mosso *(pyoo MOHS-soh)* [It.] A tempo marking that indicates "more motion," or faster.

poco *(POH-koh)* [It.] Little; for example *poco dim.* means "a little softer."

poco a poco *(POH-koh ah POH-koh)* [It.] Little by little; for example, *poco a poco cresc.* means "little by little increase in volume."

polyphony *(pah-LIH-fun-nee)* [Gk.] Literally, "many sounding." A type of music in which there are two or more different melodic lines being sung or played at the same time. Polyphony was refined during the Renaissance, and this period is sometimes called the "golden age of polyphony."

polyrhythms A technique in which several different rhythms are performed at the same time.

portamento A smooth and rapid glide from one note to another, executed continuously.

psalm A sacred song or hymn. Specifically, one of the 150 Psalms in the Bible.

presto *(PREH-stoh)* [It.] Very fast.

program music A descriptive style of music composed to relate or illustrate a specific incident, situation or drama; the form of the piece is often dictated or influenced by the nonmusical program. This style commonly occurs in music composed during the Romantic period.

Q

quarter note A note that represents one beat of sound when the quarter note receives the beat.

quarter note triplet Three equal divisions of a half note.

quarter rest A rest that represents one beat of silence when the quarter note receives the beat.

quartet A group of four singers or instrumentalists.

R

rallentando *(rall.)* *(rahl-en-TAHN-doh)* [It.] Meaning to "perform more and more slowly." *See also* ritard.

refrain A repeated section at the end of each phrase or verse in a song. Also known as a *chorus*.

register, vocal A term used for different parts of the singer's range, such as head register, or head voice (high notes); and chest register, or chest voice (low notes).

relative minor scale A minor scale that shares the same key signature as its corresponding major scale. Both scales share the same half steps: between *mi* and *fa,* and *ti* and *do.*

Renaissance period The historical period in Western civilization from 1430 to 1600.

repeat sign A symbol that indicates that a section of music should be (:‖) repeated.

repetition The restatement of a musical idea; repeated pitches; repeated "A" section in ABA form.

requiem *(REK-wee-ehm)* [Lt.] Literally, "rest." A mass written and performed to honor the dead and comfort the living.

resolution The progression of chords or notes from the dissonant to the consonant, or point of rest.

resonance Reinforcement and intensification of sound by vibration.

rest A symbol used in music notation to indicate silence.

rhythm The combination of long and short notes and rests in music. These may move with the beat, faster than the beat or slower than the beat.

ritard *(rit.) (ree-TAHRD)* [It.] A tempo marking that indicates to gradually get slower.

Romantic period The historical period in Western civilization from 1820 to 1900

Romantic style In music history, the Romantic period dates from 1820–1900, following the Classical period. The word *romantic* (in music, as in art and literature) has to do with romance, imagination, strangeness and fantasy. Music composed in the *Romantic style*, when compared with the balance and restraint of the *Classical style*, is freer and more subjective, with increasing use of chromaticism.

rondo form A form in which a repeated section is separated by several contrasting sections.

rote The act of learning a song by hearing it over and over again.

round *See* canon.

rubato *(roo-BAH-toh)* [It.] The freedom to slow down and/or speed up the tempo without changing the overall pulse of a piece of music.

S

sacred music Music associated with religious services or themes.

scale A group of pitches that are sung or played in succession and are based on a particular home tone, or keynote.

scat singing An improvisational style of singing that uses nonsense syllables instead of words. It was made popular by jazz trumpeter Louis Armstrong.

Schubertiad Gatherings held in the homes of Viennese middle-class families; they featured amateur performances of songs and instrumental works by Franz Schubert (1797–1828).

score A notation showing all parts of a musical ensemble, with the parts stacked vertically and rhythmically aligned.

sea chantey A song sung by sailors, usually in rhythm with their work.

second The interval between two consecutive degrees of the diatonic scale.

secular music Music not associated with religious services or themes.

sempre *(SEHM-preh)* [It.] Always, continually.

sempre accelerando *(sempre accel.)* *(SEHM-preh ahk-chel)* [It.] A term that indicates to gradually increase the tempo of a piece or section of music.

sequence A successive musical pattern that begins on a higher or lower pitch each time it is repeated.

serenata [It.] A large-scale musical work written in honor of a special occasion. Generally performed in the evening or outside, it is often based on a mythological theme.

seventh The interval between the first and seventh degrees of the diatonic scale.

sforzando *(sfohr-TSAHN-doh)* [It.] A sudden strong accent on a note or chord. (*sfz*)

sharp A symbol that raises the pitch of a given note one half step. (♯)

sight-sing Reading and singing music at first sight.

simile *(sim.) (SIM-ee-leh)* [It.] To continue the same way.

simple meter Any meter in which the quarter note receives the beat, and the division of the beat is based on two eighth notes. 2/4, 3/4 and 4/4 are examples of simple meter.

singing posture The way one sits or stands while singing.

Singspiel *(ZEENG-shpeel)* [Ger.] A light German opera with spoken dialogue; e.g., Mozart's *The Magic Flute*.

sixteenth note A note that represents one quarter beat of sound when the quarter note receives the beat. Four sixteenth notes equal one beat of sound when the quarter note receives the beat.

sixteenth rest A rest that represents one quarter beat of silence when the quarter note receives the beat. Four sixteenth rests equal one beat of silence when the quarter note receives the beat.

skipwise motion The movement from a given note to another note that is two or more notes above or below it on the staff.

slur A curved line placed over or under a group of notes to indicate that they are to be performed without a break.

solfège syllables Pitch names using *do, re, mi, fa, sol, la, ti, do,* etc.

solo One person singing or playing an instrument alone.

sonata-allegro form A large ABA form consisting of three sections: exposition, development and recapitulation. This form was made popular during the Classical period.

soprano The highest-sounding female voice.

sostenuto (*SAHS-tuh-noot-oh*) [It.] The sustaining of a tone or the slackening of tempo.

sotto voce In a quiet, subdued manner; "under" the voice.

spirito (*SPEE-ree-toh*) [It.] Spirited; for example, *con spirito* ("with spirit").

spiritual Songs that were first sung by African American slaves, usually based on biblical themes or stories.

staccato (*stah-KAH-toh*) [It.] A short and detached style of singing or playing.

staff A series of five horizontal lines and four spaces on which notes are written. A staff is like a ladder. Notes placed higher on the staff sound higher than notes placed lower on the staff.

stage presence A performer's overall appearance on stage, including enthusiasm, facial expression and posture.

staggered breathing In ensemble singing, the practice of planning breaths so that no two singers take a breath at the same time, thus creating the overall effect of continuous singing.

staggered entrances A technique in which different parts and voices enter at different times.

stanza A section in a song in which the words change on each repeat. Also known as a verse.

stepwise motion The movement from a given note to another note that is directly above or below it on the staff.

straight tone A singing technique that uses minimal vocal vibrato.

strophe A verse or stanza in a song.

strophic A form in which the melody repeats while the words change from verse to verse.

style The particular character of a musical work, often indicated by words at the beginning of a composition, telling the performer the general manner in which the piece is to be performed.

subdominant chord A chord built on the fourth note of a scale. In a major scale, this chord uses the notes *fa, la* and *do,* and it may be called the **IV** ("four") chord, since it is based on the fourth note of the major scale, or *fa.* In a minor scale, this chord uses the notes *re, fa* and *la,* and it may be called the **iv** ("four") chord, since it is based on the fourth note of the minor scale, or *re.*

subito (sub.) (*SOO-bee-toh*) [It.] Suddenly.

subject The main musical idea in a fugue.

suspension   The holding over of one or more musical tones in a chord into the following chord, producing a momentary discord.

swell   A somewhat breathy, sudden crescendo. It is often used in gospel music.

swing rhythms   Rhythms in which the second eighth note of each beat is played or sung like the last third of triplet, creating an uneven, "swing" feel. A style often found in jazz and blues. Swing rhythms are usually indicated at the beginning of a song or section.

syllabic   *See* syllabic singing.

syllabic singing   A style of text setting in which one syllable is sung on each note.

syllabic stress   The stressing of one syllable over another.

symphonic poem   A single-movement work for orchestra, inspired by a painting, play or other literary or visual work. Franz Liszt was a prominent composer of symphonic poems. Also known as a tone poem.

symphony   A large-scale work for orchestra.

syncopation   The placement of accents on a weak beat or a weak portion of the beat, or on a note or notes that normally do not receive extra emphasis.

synthesizer   A musical instrument that produces sounds electronically, rather than by the physical vibrations of an acoustic instrument.

T

tag   The ending of a barbershop song, usually the last four to eight bars, often considered the best chords in the song.

tamburo *(tahm-BOO-roh)*   [It.] A two-headed drum played horizontally on the player's lap.

tempo   Terms in music that indicate how fast or slow to sing or play.

tempo I or tempo primo   *See a tempo.* **tenor** The highest-sounding male vo

tenor   The highest-sounding male voice.

tenuto *(teh-NOO-toh)*   [It.] A symbol placed above or below a given note indicating that the note should receive stress and/or that its value should be slightly extended.

terraced dynamics   Sudden and abrupt dynamic changes between loud and soft.

tessitura *(tehs-see-TOO-rah)*   [It.] The average highness or lowness in pitch of a vocal piece.

text   Words, usually set in a poetic style, that express a central thought, idea or narrative.

texture   The thickness of the different layers of horizontal and vertical sounds.

theme   A musical idea, usually a melody.

theme and variation form   A musical form in which variations of the basic theme make up the composition.

third   An interval of two pitches that are three notes apart on a staff.

tie   A curved line used to connect two or more notes of the same pitch together in order to make one longer note.

tied notes   Two or more notes of the same pitch connected together with a tie in order to make one longer note.

timbre   The tone quality of a person's voice or musical instrument.

time signature   The set of numbers at the beginning of a piece of music. The top number indicates the number of beats per measure. The bottom number indicates the kind of note that receives the beat. Time signature is sometimes called *meter signature.*

to coda   Skip to (⊕) or CODA.

tonality   The relationship of a piece of music to its *keynote* (tonic).

tone color   That which distinguishes the voice or tone of one singer or instrument from another; for example, a soprano from an alto, or a flute from a clarinet. *See also* timbre.

tonic chord A chord built on the home tone, or keynote, of a scale. In a major scale, this chord uses the notes *do, mi* and *sol*, and it may be called the **I** ("one") chord, since it is based on the first note of the major scale, or *do*. In a minor scale, this chord uses the notes *la, do* and *mi*, and it may be called the **i** ("one") chord, since it is based on the first note of the minor scale, or *la*.

treble clef A clef that generally indicates notes that sound higher than middle C.

trio A group of three singers or instrumentalists with usually one on a part.

triple A grouping of notes in equal sets of three.

triplet A group of notes in which three notes of equal duration are sung in the time normally given to two notes of equal duration.

troppo *(TROHP-oh)* [It.] Too much; for example, *allegro non troppo* ("not too fast").

tutti *(TOO-tee)* [It.] Meaning "all" or "together."

twelve-tone music A type of music that uses all twelve tones of the scale equally. Developed in the early twentieth century, Arnold Schoenberg is considered to be the pioneer of this style of music.

two-part music A type of music in which two different parts are sung or played.

U

unison All parts singing or playing the same notes at the same time.

upbeat One or more notes of a melody that occur before the first barline or which fall on a weak beat that leans toward the strong beat.

V

vaccin An instrument consisting of one or two sections of bamboo, blown with the lips like one would play the mouthpiece of a brass instrument. Also called a *bambou*.

variation A modification of a musical idea, usually after its initial appearance in a piece.

vibrato *(vee-BRAH-toh)* [It.] A fluctuation of pitch on a single note, especially by singers and string players.

villancico *(bee-ahn-SEE-koh)* [Sp.] A Spanish musical and poetic form consisting of several verses linked by a refrain. In modern-day Spain and Latin America, the term *villancico* usually means simply "Christmas carol."

vivace *(vee-VAH-chay)* [It.] Very fast; lively.

vocal jazz A popular style of music characterized by strong prominent meter, improvisation and dotted or syncopated patterns. Sometimes sung *a cappella*.

W

whole note A note that represents four beats of sound when the quarter note receives the beat. o

whole rest A rest that represents four beats of silence when the quarter note receives the beat. ▬

whole step The combination of two successive half steps.

word painting A technique in which the music reflects the meaning of the words.

word stress The act of singing important parts of the text in a more accented style than the other parts.

Classified Index

A Cappella

Domine Fili Unigenite 48
Hoj, Hura, Hoj 176
O Vos Omnes 198
Overture to *Die Zauberflöte* 82
See The Gipsies 232
Sing A New Song 240
The Star-Spangled Banner 32
Vere Languores Nostros 76
When I Fall In Love 259

Composers

**Giovanni Pierluigi da Palestrina
(1525–1594)**
Domine Fili Unigenite 48

Antonio Lotti (1667–1740)
Vere Languores Nostros 76

Antonio Caldara (c. 1670–1736)
Sebben, crudele 220

Wolfgang Amadeus Mozart (1756–1791)
Overture to *Die Zauberflöte* 82

Johannes Brahms (1833–1897)
Die Schwestern 94

Gustav Holst (1874–1934)
Homeland 36

Mary Goetze
Fire 104

Moses Hogan (1975–2003)
Music Down In My Soul 186

Folk

African American Spiritual
Didn't My Lord Deliver Daniel 20
Go Where I Send Thee! 66
Music Down In My Soul 186

American
He's Gone Away 170

Dominican Republic
El Pambiche Lento 152

Hungarian
See The Gipsies 232

French Canadian
Ah! si mon moine voulait danser! . . 138

Foreign Language

Czech
Hoj, Hura, Hoj 176

French
Ah! si mon moine voulait danser! . . 138

German
Die Schwestern 94

Hebrew
Shiru 10

Italian
Sebben, crudele 220

Latin
Domine Fili Unigenite 48
O Vos Omnes 198
Vere Languores Lostros 76

Spanish
El Pambiche Lento 152

Gospel

Go Where I Send Thee! 66
Music Down In My Soul 186

Instruments

Clarinet
Sing A Song Of Sixpence 246

Percussion
Ah! si mon moine voulait danser! . . 138
El Pambiche Lento 152

Two Pianos
Psalm 100 204

Music & History

Renaissance
Domine Fili Unigenite 48

Baroque
Sebben, crudele 220
Vere Languores Nostros 76

Classical
Overture to *Die Zauberflöte* 82

Romantic
Die Schwestern 94

Contemporary
Homeland 36
Music Down In My Soul 186

Poetry

Die Schwestern 94
Fire 104
Homeland 36
In Time Of Silver Rain 2
Sing A Song Of Sixpence 246

Seasonal, Patriotic

Go Where I Send Thee! 66
Homeland 36
In Time Of Silver Rain 2
The Star-Spangled Banner 32
Through Winter's WIndow 56

Vocal Jazz

Go Where I Send Thee! 66
Overture to *Die Zauberflöte* 82
When I Fall In Love 259

Listening Selections

O Magnum Mysterium
    Tomás Luis de Victoria 119

Canzon XV
    Giovanni Gabrieli 119

Te Deum (excerpt)
    Henry Purcell 123

"Spring" (First Movement)
    from *The Four Seasons*
    Antonio Vivaldi 123

"Gloria" from *Coronation Mass*
    Wolfgang Amadeus Mozart 127

Symphony #100 in G Major
    Second Movement
    Franz Joseph Haydn 127

"How Lovely Is Thy Dwelling Place"
    from *A German Requiem*
    Johannes Brahms 131

Symphony #5 in C Minor
    First Movement
    Ludwig van Beethoven 131

"Laudamus Te" from *Gloria*
    Francis Poulenc 135

"Street in a Frontier Town"
    from *Billy the Kid*
    Aaron Copland 135

Index of Songs and Spotlights

Ah! si mon moine voulait danser! 138
Didn't My Lord Deliver Daniel 20
Die Schwestern 94
Domine Fili Unigenite 48
El Pambiche Lento 152
Fire 104
Go Where I Send Thee! 66
He's Gone Away 170
Hoj, Hura, Hoj 176
Homeland 36
In Time Of Silver Rain 2
Music Down In My Soul 186
O Vos Omnes 198
Overture To *Die Zauberflöte* 82
Psalm 100 204
Sebben, crudele 220
See The Gipsies 232
Shiru 10
Sing A New Song 240
Sing A Song Of Sixpence 246
The Star-Spangled Banner 32
Through Winter's Window 56
Vere Languores Nostros 76
When I Fall In Love 259

Spotlights
Arranging 151
Careers In Music 136
Concert Etiquette 114
Gospel Music 75
Improvisation 203
Posture & Breath Management 9
Physiology Of Singing 93
Physiology Of The Voice 65
Vocal Health 185
Vocal Jazz 231

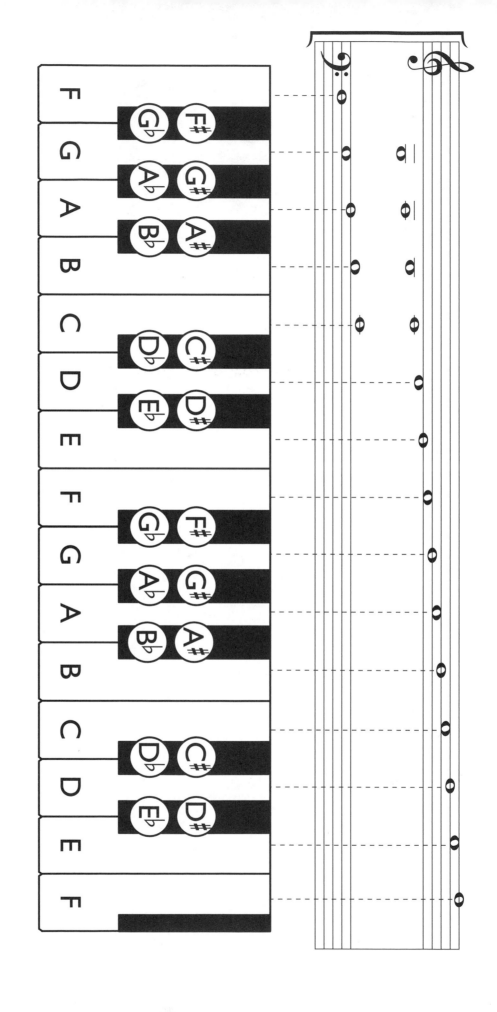